OUTING THE TRUTH ABOUT SEXUAL ORIENTATION

BRAD BOWINS, M.D., F.R.C.P.(C)

Science & Humanities Press

Saint Charles Missouri USA

ISBN 9781596301023

Library of Congress Control Number: 2016930936

Science & Humanities Press

Saint Charles Missouri USA

sciencehumanitiespress.com

DEDICATION

To my children, Emma, Mark, & Breanna, my wife Lynne, and my parents, Mildred & Earl.

TABLE OF CONTENTS

INTRODUCTION: WHAT IS SEXUAL ORIENTATION ALL ABOUT?

Sexual orientation is a topic of relevance to everyone, even those who are asexual lacking any interest in either sex. The reason why is simple—Sexual orientation forms a crucial component of how us humans, a very social species, interact with each other. People categorize others on the basis of being gay, straight, or bisexual. In addition, sexual orientation usually occupies a prominent position in the way that we view ourselves. Despite how important the topic is to each of us, most people have a very limited understanding of what constitutes sexual orientation. It is a complex topic involving a number of components, and information about it is quite convoluted and confusing. Consequently, it is difficult for people to shrink it down into a meaningful and accurate picture, capable of improving how they relate to others and view themselves. Whenever there is confusion and misunderstanding negative feelings and behaviors typically follow, and this is certainly true in the case of sexual orientation. People frequently feel guilty and ashamed if they are not part of the heterosexual majority, and resentment leading to discrimination and persecution of gays and bisexuals is common in much of the world.

As a psychiatrist having worked with many non-heterosexual individuals, I have seen the emotional suffering that many gay and bisexual people experience, and also the discrimination and persecution that occurs. One reason for writing this book is to provide an enlightened and comprehensive understanding of sexual

1

orientation that will hopefully reduce discrimination and persecution, and help people feel better about their sexual orientation. Another reason is to resolve an intriguing evolutionary paradox, the solution having enormous relevance for what sexual orientation actually represents. Evolution occurs when genes that favor reproduction, or at least do not hinder it, are passed onto succeeding generations, with genes that most aid in reproduction being those most passed on—Natural selection. Homosexuality represents an evolutionary paradox, because how can behavior not leading to reproduction, and seemingly actually blocking it, possibly evolve?

If homosexual individuals do not mate with members of the other-sex there is no chance that their genes, including ones for being gay, will be passed on. However, homosexuality is alive and well and shows no signs of fading. The answer uncovered and presented here fully resolves this evolutionary paradox, and in the process provides a very clear and comprehensive picture of what constitutes sexual orientation. You will have to read on and see what the answer is, but suffice it to say that homosexual and heterosexual orientations do not in and of themselves represent true occurrences, but only partially accurate descriptions of naturally occurring events, despite what we all believe. A major reason why so many theories of sexual orientation fail is that they are based on the faulty assumption that homosexuality and heterosexuality are real entities.

The book provides readers with the background necessary for understanding sexual orientation in chapters pertaining to discrimination and persecution, psychological theories, biological theories, and animal homosexuality. The fascinating topic of "homosexual" behavior in animals, in combination with the failure of all existing psychological and biological theories to account for the evolutionary paradox, sets the stage for how sexual orientation needs to be understood. The chapters that follow provide all the pieces for an improved and comprehensive understanding of sexual orientation. We will look at how sexual orientation is organized dimensionally, the functions served by these dimensions, how they can be activated or deactivated by circumstances, the powerful influence of erotic fantasy, and the impressive role that social construction plays in "homosexuality" and "heterosexuality." Utilizing the perspective presented, the last core chapter addresses the intriguing issue of transgender, transforming it from a highly complex topic into one that is actually quite straightforward. The ultimate goal of this book is to improve our understanding and way of conceptualizing sexual orientation, such that we can get over our other and self-directed resentments and embrace who we really are as sexual beings.

DISCRIMINATION

A key motivation for writing this book is the enormous amount of discrimination against homosexual individuals that I have seen in my practice as a psychiatrist. A disproportionate number of people seeing psychiatrists have experienced trauma in their early or even later life. Frequently, trauma arises from bullying and discrimination, commonly based on perceived sexual orientation. The typical pattern that I have encountered with homosexual individuals is that during childhood or the teenage years, when peers realized they were different, the name calling often starts. Names like fag, gay, queer, and dyke, ensue often spreading like wildfire amongst the larger peer group. Ostracism, meaning exclusion from normal activities of the peer group typically occur, such as not being invited to parties or asked to be on a team. The targeted individual already realizing that something is "different" about them feels more unusual and unwanted, an emotional state leading to further social withdrawal. Often this discrimination is more difficult to cope with when the person is not yet aware that they are "gay," because others seem to be seeing something in them they cannot understand. Even when they are self-aware there is typically no one to turn to, given that other homosexual individuals are doing their best to cover it up for fear of attacks. In some instances actual physical and sexual assaults transpire worsening the emotional trauma experienced.

For a number of homosexual people the problems more or less resolve away from their school years, as they "come out" and relate to homosexual and more

4

understanding heterosexual peers. However, often the problems intensify due to rejection by family members, even in some instances to the point of being disowned by parents and siblings. If a person decides not to "come out," there are numerous complications, such as continually explaining to relatives and friends why there is no partner, and why they are not married. Many religions, despite opposing discrimination against their own followers, openly or covertly engage in bias against people with a homosexual or bisexual orientation. I had one patient who was strongly pushed into therapy to resolve his "gay issue" as a condition of remaining in the church. For many individuals who want to remain in their given church community the only option is to hide their sexual orientation, even to the point of marrying an other-sex person within the church, and leading a secretive closeted lifestyle on the side. Occupational discrimination is often a major problem, particularly in more traditionally masculine jobs such as engineering. Careers can falter and crash based on a person being openly gay, and I have seen many such individuals hide all signs of their sexual orientation.

It might be argued that my experience is based on a relatively small sample size, and that discrimination and bullying due to sexual orientation is actually not a real problem. Well let us see what studies reveal. Research by Saewyc and colleagues—Hazards of stigma: The sexual and physical abuse of gay, lesbian, and bisexual adolescents in the United States and Canada—produced some shocking findings. Surveys of high school students in both countries formed the database. The prevalence of sexual abuse or forced intercourse experienced by heterosexual girls ranged from 14-27%, uncomfortably high, but low compared to that experienced by those identifying as lesbian or bisexual. Sexual abuse or forced intercourse for lesbians ranged from 18-43%, and 24-40% for bisexuals! Heterosexual boys experienced sexual abuse or forced intercourse in the range of 3-6%. For boys identifying as being gay the range was 17-31%, and for bisexual boys 15-31%! These numbers are incredibly high and this is for sexual assault, a crime inflicting enormous psychological, and often physical, trauma.

The findings for bisexuals surprise many people, given that they do function in heterosexual relationships. In my own practice I have noted that in many instances people identifying as bisexual have an even tougher go than homosexuals, because discrimination can come from both heterosexuals and homosexuals, as odd as this sounds. The reason largely has to do with how sexual orientation is dichotomized in our society into hetero and homo categories. The presence of both in one individual is difficult to process, due to how we see it in either/or terms. Many bisexuals are viewed as really being homosexual, but not yet admitting it. Saewyc and colleagues point out that bisexual boys are ten times more likely than their heterosexual peers to experience sexual abuse! These researchers comment that a history of sexual or physical trauma is highly predictive of adolescent risk behaviors, including substance abuse, dangerous sexual behaviors, and even suicide attempts. Hence, the impact of sexual abuse goes far beyond the person's emotional reaction to the actual event, and can have a lifelong impact.

You might be thinking that these poor unfortunate teenage victims of sexual abuse, including forced intercourse, are sympathized with given the trauma they have experienced. Well maybe the heterosexual ones, but based on a study by Christopher Lyons titled, Stigma or sympathy? Attributions of fault to hate crime victim and offenders, it appears that non-heterosexual victims are likely to be blamed. He discovered that gay and lesbian victims are blamed at a much higher rate than are heterosexual victims. So not only does the homosexual or bisexual person suffer from the sexual abuse, they are often blamed for it! Talk about adding insult to injury, or more precisely injury to injury. Lyons found that blaming behavior depends on the observer's attitude towards homosexuals, with more negative attitudes producing more blaming. Interestingly, the study revealed that when gays or lesbians victims made eye contact with the attacker or verbally responded with a question or obscenity, the person was more likely to be blamed than heterosexual victims who responded in this way. Blaming of homosexual victims for the attack was maximal when observers witness displays of affection just prior to the attack, such as hand holding and kissing. Such displays of affection did not impact on blaming when observed for heterosexual victims prior to an attack.

Several lines of research reveal that hate crimes involving adult homosexual, bisexual, and transgender victims are very common. The United States Federal Bureau Of Investigation (FBI) tracks hate crimes reported by law enforcement agencies. In 2011, 6,222 hate crimes involving 7,254 offences were reported. Offences included intimidation, assault, rape, murder, and vandalism. Sexual orientation bias accounted for 20.8% compared to 19.8% religious, 11.6% ethnicity/national origin, and 0.9% disability. Racial motivation was the basis for 46.9%, not surprising considering the long-standing history of friction between blacks and whites in the United States. Hence, sexual discrimination was the main cause of hate crimes other than for those racially motivated. It is important to note that these are for serious crimes having a major impact on the victim's life. Furthermore, sexual orientation hate crimes are more likely than any other

7

type of hate crime to be targeted at the person rather than property, and far more likely than those based on religion. Regarding who was targeted, 56.7% were against homosexual males, 11.1% were directed at homosexual females, and the rest at homosexuals generally or transgender individuals.

Many victims of sexual orientation hate crimes do not report the incident to police partly based on fear of being "outed," or of not being treated fairly. Edward Dunbar's study, Race, gender, and sexual orientation in hate crime victimization: Identity politics or identity risk?, sheds light on the reporting issue. He discovered that only 66% of lesbians and 74% of gay men report victimization to law enforcement agencies. Consequently, many hate crimes against homosexuals are not reported to the police. Race interacts with the tendency to report the crime with only 52% of black lesbians reporting such an occurrence, in contrast to 81% of gay white men. The former group, appear to surmise that they will not be treated seriously, while white gay men of generally higher socioeconomic status feel more confident that the offence will be dealt with.

The National Coalition of Anti-Violence Projects found that from 1998 to 2011, when statistics started to be recorded, that 2011 was the highest for hate crimes against non-heterosexuals. The rate of hate crimes experienced by non-heterosexuals is at least twice the rate encountered by heterosexuals. The 2012 report by the coalition also found that non-heterosexual youth and young adults were 2.41 times as likely to experience physical violence, compared to non-heterosexuals 30 years and older. This is an interesting finding as it suggests that the preponderance of physical assaults against non-heterosexuals occurs in the younger age groups, who arguably might be more vulnerable to the impact of trauma.

Statistics are one thing, but real life examples provide graphic illustrations of what homosexual and bisexual people experience. The situation is if anything worse for transgender individuals with examples provided in the transgender chapter. In reading these examples imagine that you, one of your children, relatives, or friends is the victim. They are taken from History of violence against LGBT people in the United States, Wikipedia starting in the 1970's. On July 5, 1978 a gang of youths armed with baseball bats and tree branches entered Central Park with the intent of attacking homosexuals. Victims, including former figure skater Dick Button, were assaulted randomly. On November 27, 1978 Harvey Milk, the openly gay San Francisco city supervisor, and major George Moscone, were assassinated by political rival Dan White at San Francisco City Hall. Outrage over White's short seven-year prison sentence, triggered the White Night riots. September 7, 1979 Robert Allen Taylor was stabbed to death near Loring Park in Minneapolis. His murderer told a local reporter, "I don't like gays. Okay?"

Rebecca Wight and her partner, Claudia Brenner, were hiking and camping along the Appalachian Trail on May 13, 1988. Stephen Roy Carr, who happened to be on the trail at the same time, witnessed them having sex. He shot them later explaining that he became enraged. Rebecca Wight died of her injuries. I have a gay patient who in the late 1980's shared a city apartment and home in the country with his male partner. The patient I see had to remain in the city for work and his lover decided to stay in the country. Two men who heard that a male child was sexually assaulted in the region, apparently assumed it had to be the only openly gay man in the area, my patient's partner. They forcibly entered the country home

9

and killed him, after what was described as a very protracted and bloody fight. He did not even know the child in question, and had never assaulted a child. Those who hate homosexuals often assume that they prey on children, but the frequency of child abuse is no higher than with heterosexuals.

On July 2, 1990 Julio Rivera was murdered in New York City by two men simply because he was gay. They beat him with a hammer and also stabbed him. U.S. Navy Petty Officer Allen Schindler was stomped to death by a shipmate on October 27, 1992. Schindler had repeatedly complained about anti-gay harassment aboard ship. His case was a key focus in the gays in the military debate, resulting in the "Don't ask, don't tell" bill, whereby the armed forces could not ask if a person was gay and the person was not to tell. If it became known the person was gay he or she would have to leave the armed forces. On October 7, 1998 Matthew Sheppard a gay student in Laramie Wyoming was tortured, beaten, tied to a fence, and abandoned. He remained in this horrible state for 18 hours before he was found. Less than a week later he died from his injuries. Russell Arthur Henderson and Aaron James McKinney are both serving two consecutive life sentences for the crime.

With the new millennium there does not appear to be an enlightened perspective on how homosexuals should be treated, at least based on hate crimes. On July 3, 2000 Arther "J.R." Warren was punched and kicked to death in Grant Town, West Virginia by two teenage boys. They believed that Warren had spread a rumor that he and one of the boys, David Allen Parker, had a sexual relationship. The two teenagers ran over Warren's body to disguise the murder as a hit-and-run. Parker was sentenced to 15 years and his accomplice, Jared Wilson, to 20 years. Sakia Gunn, a 15-year old black lesbian was

10

murdered in Newark, New Jersey, May 11, 2003. While Gunn and her friends were waiting for a bus, two men propositioned them. When the girls rejected the advances declaring that they were lesbian, the men attacked. Richard McCullough fatally stabbed Gunn. He ended up receiving a 20-year prison sentence.

A particularly gruesome attack against a "down-and-out" gay male occurred on October 2, 2004. Daniel Fetty, a gay hearing-impaired homeless man, was attacked by several assailants in Waverly Ohio. He was beaten, kicked, shoved nude into a garbage bin, impaled with a stick, and left for dead. It took him a day to die of his injuries. Three men received sentences ranging from 7-years to life. On February 2, 2006, 18-year old Jacob Robida entered a bar in New Bedford, Massachusetts. After confirming that it was indeed a gay bar he attacked patrons with a hatchet and handgun, wounding three. He took his own life a few days later. On February 27, 2007, Andrew Anthos, a 72-year old disabled gay man was beaten with a lead pipe in Detroit, Michigan, by a man who was shouting anti-gay names at him. Anthos died 10 days after the attack. A 25-year old gay man, Nathaniel Salerno, was attacked by four men on a Metro train in Washington, DC. They called him "faggot" while beating him.

On November 7, 2008 the home of openly gay Melvin Whistlehunt in Newton, North Carolina, was destroyed by arsonists. Homophobic graffiti was spray-painted on the back of the house. Demonstrating how cultural traditions can get confused with homosexual actions, and with fatal consequences, is the case of two Ecuadorean brothers. On December 7, 2008, Romel Sucuzhanya, a 31-year old straight man and his brother, Jose, were walking arm-in-arm on a Brooklyn New York street. This behavior is normal for brothers in their culture. They were attacked for appearing gay, with Romel dying of his injuries. A 28-year old lesbian was kidnapped in Richmond California on December 12, 2008 and gang raped by four men who made homophobic remarks during the attack. On April 6, 2009 Carl Joseph Walker-Hoover, an 11-year old child in Springfield Massachusetts hanged himself because he was bullied at school by peers who said he acted feminine and was gay.

In another military case Seaman August Provost was found shot to death and burned at his guard post at Camp Pendleton on June 30, 2009. Provost had been harassed due to his sexual orientation. Military leaders believe that the "Don't ask, don't tell" policy prevented Provost from seeking help. Even a university campus at night is not safe, or was not for Quinn Matney attending university in North Carolina. He was taking an evening stroll on April 4, 2011 when an unidentified man branded him as gay and burned his wrists. On June 23, 2012, 19-year old Mollie Olgin and her 18-year old girlfriend, Kristene Chapa, were both found shot in the head near Violet Andrews Park in Portland Texas. Olgin died at the scene but Chapa survived. On May 17, 2013 Mark Carson, a 32-year old gay black man, was shot to death in Greenwich Village, New York. Carson was walking with a friend when another man trailed and taunted them. Anti-gay remarks were made and one was asked, "You want to die tonight?" Elliot Morales has been charged with murder.

The examples provided demonstrate that a great deal of hatred is directed towards homosexual men and women of all races. The examples also reveal that in many instances there is no relationship between the attacker/s and victim/s. In some cases, it is just a matter of being in the wrong place at the wrong time. A random person or persons who resent homosexuals can launch an attack. In other instances, such as those involving military personnel, the problem can be very systemic and the attacker knows the victim. Often the degree of violence is so over the top that it is clear that many people view homosexuality as a completely alien entity that needs to be taken care of, and in a very definitive way.

More subtle negative and biased treatment of homosexual and bisexual individuals frequently transpires in the workplace, with research showing that it is a definite force to be contended with. The Catalyst Knowledge Center provides statistics based on independent studies pertaining to lesbian (L), gay (G), bisexual (B), and transgender (T) workplace issues. The results clearly indicate that these individuals are not treated fairly. 37.7% of "out" LGB employees have experienced discrimination, compared to 27.1% of all such employees including those who are not "out." Furthermore, 38.2% of "out" LGB employees have experienced harassment, compared to 27.1% of all LGB employees. These statistics support the strategy practiced by many homosexual and bisexual individuals of keeping their sexual orientation hidden.

According to the Catalyst Knowledge Center, 67% of LGBT employees do not report anti-LGBT remarks to human resources or management, and certainly not those remaining closeted in the workplace. 15-43% of gay and transgender employees have experience some form of either discrimination or harassment in the workplace. 8-17% were either not hired or fired due to their sexual orientation, and 10-28% were not promoted because they were gay or transgender. Transgender individuals are particularly discriminated against, with 97% having experienced harassment or mistreatment in the workplace, and 47% fired, not hired, or not advanced due to their gender identity. Amazingly, 7-41% of gay and transgender employees have been verbally or physically assaulted, or had their workplace vandalized! LGBT individuals then have much more stress to contend with in the typical workplace setting than do heterosexual individuals. Discrimination against these LGBT individuals occurs, despite anti-discrimination legislation and pro-gay employment policies present in many corporations and workplace settings.

So far the discussion of persecution and discrimination targeting those who are not heterosexual has been North American based. In much of the world the situation is vastly worse with no rights for LGBT individuals, and even formalized persecution involving the possibility of jail time or execution, if caught engaging in a homosexual relationship. Five countries still prescribe capital punishment for homosexuals including Iran, Mauritania, the Republic of Sudan, Saudi Arabia, and Yemen. Former Iranian President Mahmoud Ahmadinejad boldly claimed that Iran does not have homosexuals, because they are executed. Graphic pictures of homosexual men being executed in Iran can be readily found online if anyone is in doubt. In addition to the five mentioned countries parts of Somalia and Nigeria still execute homosexuals, and southern Sudan is considering raising the 10-year prison sentence to capital punishment. Many of these countries are highly repressive in general, including against freedom of expression.

Europe makes a good comparison to the North American data, given its generally progressive nature regarding human rights. The largest study to date of discrimination and persecution is the 2012 European Union lesbian, gay, bisexual and transgender survey. Information was collected from a staggering 93,079 LGBT individuals residing in the EU and Croatia. The survey consisted of an anonymous online questionnaire beginning with screening questions to establish a person's eligibility. Only those 18 years and older who identified as lesbian, gay, bisexual, or transgender, and living in the EU or Croatia were eligible. The questionnaire consisted of 10 sections designed to assess the respondents' background, and experiences and views of discrimination, violence, and harassment. Of the 93,079 respondents 15,236 (16%) were lesbian, 57,448 (62%) gay men, 6,424 (7%) bisexual women, 7,200 (8%) bisexual men, and 6,771 (7%) transgender. Regarding age, 28,110 (30%) were 18-24, 39,939 (43%) 25-39, 20,236 (22%) 40-54, and 4,794 (5%) 55+. Hence, all LGBT categories and age groups were well represented, although the experience of older individuals perhaps less well so.

The EU survey questionnaire covered many experiences and the results are very revealing. They are also quite consistent with North American data. Respondents were asked who felt discriminated against or harassed in the last 12 months on the grounds of sexual orientation. Answering in the affirmative were 55% lesbians, 45% gay men, 47% bisexual women, 36% bisexual men, and 46% transgender. The lowest rate was for the Netherlands (30%) and highest rate for Lithuania (61%), with the EU average 47%. Note that these values are for the last 12 months only. Workplace discrimination and harassment is a major problem for LGBT people, and the survey assessed those who felt discriminated against in the last 12 months when looking for a job and/or at work because of being LGBT. The results revealed lesbians 21%, gay men 20%, bisexual women 16%, bisexual men 16%, and transgender 29%. The lowest rate was for Denmark (11%) and the highest rate for Cyprus (30%), with the EU average 20%. Respondents who felt discriminated against in the last 12 months in areas other than employment because of being LGBT, consisted of 39% lesbians, 29% gay men, 34% bisexual women, 24%

bisexual men, and 38% transgender. The lowest rate was for Netherlands (20%) and the highest rate for Lithuania (42%), with the EU average 32%.

Three-quarters of all respondents believed that discrimination based on a person's sexual orientation is widespread in their country of residence. 48% of respondents were open about being LGBT to none or few of their family members, and 28% were open to none or few of their friends. Of course it could be questioned how much of a friendship it truly is if the friend is not aware or accepting of the person's sexual orientation. Only 21% were open to all of their work colleagues or schoolmates. Bisexual respondents, and in particular bisexual men, were less likely to be open to all or most of their family, friends, or colleagues/schoolmates, highlighting how this sexual orientation is often less understood and accepted than strict homosexuality. Relevant to the openness issue, while 75% of respondents indicated that it is common for different-sex couples to hold hands in public in their country, only 3% of respondents felt that it was common for same-sex couples to do so.

The EU survey assessed more specific aspects of discrimination, harassment, and violence. One area of crucial significance given the vulnerable age and limited self-esteem, is the school experience prior to 18 years of age. Respondents were asked who had heard negative comments or seen negative conduct, because a schoolmate was perceived to be LGBT during their school years before the age of 18. Answering in the affirmative were 90% lesbians, 92% gay men, 92% bisexual women, 90% bisexual men, and 90% transgender. The lowest rate was for Latvia (83%) and the highest rate for Cyprus (97%), with the EU average 91%. An interesting comment by one respondent captures the essence of the school experience—"Ten years later, I still consider being bullied

16

at school the worst form of homophobic abuse I've ever been subjected to. The constant insults for being effeminate (and therefore gay) were unbearable at school, and not much action was taken by the teachers against the bullies! Bullying forced me to remain in the closet until I reached the age of 18." Given the frequency of harsh comments indicative of negative attitudes, it is not surprising that many respondents hid their orientation during the school years. Respondents were asked about who had "always" or "often," disguised being LGBT during their schooling before the age of 18. The results are 54% lesbians, 72% gay men, 46% bisexual women, 73% bisexual men, and 70% transgender. The lowest rate was for the Czech Republic (57%) and the highest rate for Lithuania (81%), with the EU average 67%.

The EU survey results for violence and harassment are consistent with those for discrimination. In the last 5 years, 26% of all respondents were attacked or threatened with violence at home or elsewhere. The figure for transgender respondents was 35%. Respondents who said they had been attacked or threatened with violence in the last 12 months, partly or completely because they were perceived to be LGBT, consisted of 5% lesbians, 6% gay men, 4% bisexual women, 5% bisexual men, and 8% transgender. The EU average was 6%. Of the serious incidents of violence or harassment in the last five years, which happened partly or completely because the person was perceived to be LGBT, few were reported to police— Lesbians 19% violence and 5% harassment, gay men 23% violence and 6% harassment, bisexual women 15% violence and 3% harassment, bisexual men 18% violence and 5% harassment, transgender 24% violence and 8% harassment. The EU average was 22% reporting violence and 6% reporting of harassment. These figures appear to be lower than those in North America.

From the European and United States data it is clear that lesbian, gay, bisexual, and transgender individuals experience enormous discrimination, harassment, and violence based on their sexual orientation. In some countries being LGBT even warrants imprisonment or worse. In contrast, certain South Pacific cultures are quite accepting of homosexual activity, as we will see in later chapters. However, these cultures do not understand sexuality as we do based on heterosexual and homosexual dichotomous categories, and appear to have a perspective more in synch with the true nature of sexual orientation. The acceptance or rejection of homoerotic behavior unquestionably depends very much on how it is conceived by a given culture. The North American and European cultural perspective on sexual orientation, despite our "enlightened" outlook compared to many parts of the world, increases the likelihood of discrimination, harassment, and violence against non-heterosexual people. Perhaps it is time then that we become more open to a change in the status quo regarding how sexual orientation is understood.

PSYCHOLOGICAL THEORIES

Attempts to explain sexual orientation, and sexuality more generally, on the basis of psychological causation, can be divided into psychoanalytic and social learning based. Sigmund Freud developed some very complex psychodynamic notions of sexuality. His book—Three Essays On The Theory Of Sexuality—started out in 1905 as a small book, but by its sixth edition in 1925 grew to 120 pages. Freud's theories of sexuality might best be characterized as an evolving, and at times, contradictory process. As a theorist with several peer-reviewed published theories, I find many of Freud's concepts overly complex, and definitely not driven by the principle that ultimately, the truth is simple. At the core when the outer layers are peeled away the truth is probably quite simple, and a theory must capture that simplicity to be robust. Albert Einstein stated that a theory that could not be explained to a child was probably not of much use. This aligns with the so-called law of parsimony, indicating that the simplest viable explanation is typically the most accurate. Freud's simplest theory—the notion of defense mechanisms to protect vulnerable conscious system functioning—is his most robust holding up very well to empirical testing. His more complex theories, such as regarding sexuality and psychosexual stages of development, have not stood up well to close inspection. In addition, the more revisions and correcting that a theory undergoes, as with Freud's concepts of sexuality, the less likely it is to be valid.

Reflecting the complexity of Freud's theories of sexuality, it is often difficult to interpret precisely what he

19

believed. In the first essay—The sexual aberrations—he indicated that, "A disposition to perversions is an original and universal disposition of the human sexual instinct." So-called "perversions" are then apparently present amongst healthy individuals. In his second essay—Infantile sexuality—he advanced the very revolutionary notion that sexuality expresses itself in childhood and not just in adolescence. Psychosexual development starting in childhood leads to mature sexual development. This was a very important step forward because sexuality was not seen as being present in children. Freud was a very good observer, despite limitations regarding the interpretation of those observations. Watching children's behaviors he noted that "Sexual emotions and desires take many and varied forms, not all of them palpably erotic." Thumb sucking, retention of feces, and sibling rivalry are examples of not so obvious expressions, whereas childhood masturbation is a clear instance.

Many parents are shocked and even horrified to see their "innocent" toddler masturbating, often worrying that there is a serious problem and scolding the child. Rest assured that this behavior is completely natural. Children that are made to feel guilty or embarrassed about such behavior, often experience intense emotional conflicts and distress as sexual urges arise. When parents roll with the experience and make the child feel comfortable with masturbation, sexual development tends to be healthier. Compounding problems, when parents are critical of their child for masturbating they rarely talk openly about sexual matters, and the child almost never spontaneously volunteers information because a negative response is anticipated. Effectively, the child is placed in an isolated closet when it comes to sexual matters. Hence, when a new sexual experience occurs, such as true orgasm as an adolescent, the individual will be confused and worried about what is transpiring given the lack of information, and keep quiet about it instead of seeking help and reassurance from his or her parents. Obviously this is not a healthy scenario.

Sexual play amongst children is also a normal aspect of healthy sexual development, unless it progresses to the point of actual penetration. Punishing children for milder forms of such behavior can transform a childhood learning experience, important for healthy sexual functioning as an adult, into a traumatic social embarrassment. It is then very important for parents to accept childhood sexual behavior and not punish manifestations of it. A key purpose of this book is to identify what is natural for us sexually, thereby fostering a revised healthy perspective on it.

Psychosexual stages of development are a crucial aspect of Freud's theory of sexuality and psychological growth. Five stages are said to occur—Oral, anal, phallic, latency, and genital. The oral stage spans from birth to 2 years of age. In this phase sexual drives, referred to as libido or libidinal, are satisfied through the mouth, such as feeding at the mother's breast and oral exploration of the environment. Anyone at all familiar with young children has undoubtedly observed how they put everything in their mouth. This occurrence is valid, but the interpretation by Freud is questionable. A simpler explanation is that evolution has equipped us with an early ability to sample things in the environment to see if they are edible, such as learning that suckling from mother's breast satisfies hunger. This evolutionary explanation is simple and adequately accounts for the way infants explore the environment orally. There is then no need for a complex mechanism based on sexuality. Freud did however accurately describe how during the oral stage a child learns that he or she is separate from the environment, or in other words, that the person is distinct from other objects in the environment.

Freud's other psychosexual stages also involve complex and overly elaborate explanations for sexual and non-sexual occurrences. The anal (second) stage covers from 18 months to 3 years. The child's erogenous zone is said to change from the mouth to the anus. The challenge of toilet training is a crucial aspect of this stage, establishing a conflict between the Id (structure containing the mental representation of drives such as sexual and aggressive) and Ego (mental apparatus mediating between the demands of the Id and reality). The Id wants immediate gratification involving bowel discharge whenever desired, whereas the Ego requires delayed gratification and defecation on the toilet. If the Id triumphs the child learns to be self-indulgent, but if the "Superego" is too harsh the person becomes obsessive-compulsive. A more parsimonious explanation is that parents who are overly rigorous and demanding about toilet training are themselves obsessive-compulsive in nature. The child is then more likely to become obsessive-compulsive given the modeling of such behavior by the parents during toilet training, plus how any underlying genetic predisposition to obsessive-compulsive behavior will be passed on to the child. However, there does not even appear to be a true link between toilet training and the development of obsessive-compulsive behavior.

The phallic (third) stage spans the ages from 3 to 6 years. During this stage the genitals represent the primary erogenous zone, and a child becomes aware of their body and those of others. Sexual exploration occurs in games and the like. The Oedipus complex, a subject of much discussion and even humor, is the pivotal psychosexual experience. Freud believed that boys in a sense compete with their father for possession of the mother. The boy's sexual desire is directed towards the mother with jealousy and anger towards the father. The boy's Id wants to kill the father, but the more realistic Ego realizes that the father is stronger. Ambivalence arising from these conflicting motivations manifests as fear that the father will castrate the boy—Castration anxiety. Defensively the boy identifies with the father to reduce castration anxiety. The Oedipus complex is derived from an ancient Greek mythological character, Oedipus, who killed his father and sexually possessed his mother.

As pertains to girls a colleague of Freud, Carl Jung, developed the Electra complex, whereby girls are seen as developing so-called penis envy because they cannot sexually possess the mother due to not having a penis. They then redirect their sexual desires to the father, progressing to heterosexuality. The mother is identified with in the process to defend against the anxiety experienced from the Electra complex. Eventually, having a child replaces the absent penis. Freud rejected this notion and believed that there occurred a feminine or negative Oedipus conflict that was more emotional in nature, resulting in a submissive personality. Like the Oedipus complex, the Electra conflict was based on ancient Greek mythology, describing how Electra plotted with her brother to murder her mother and stepfather, in revenge for the murder of their father. Both the Oedipus and Electra complexes are very creative consistent with the mythologies they are derived from, and are clearly overly complex explanations. Undoubtedly, boys at times resent their father and daughters their mothers related to seeking attention from the other-sex parent, but this occurrence is not necessarily sexual in nature. In addition, the reverse process might be more applicable, whereby a father resents all the attention his wife gives their son, and a mother resents the attention the daughter receives from the father. Resentment from the parents is even more likely if they are insecure and immature. The child might well perceive the resentment and react with fear and anger towards the same-sex parent.

The latency stage occurs between 6 years of age and puberty. During this stage drives are hidden or latent, and gratification is delayed unlike with the oral, anal, and phallic stages. Hence, the child directs libidinal drives towards external activities such as school, friends, and hobbies. A simpler explanation for what might be occurring during this phase is that the individual is starting to learn to sublimate or redirect urges or energy that cannot be expressed directly. One of the most adaptive and mature defenses we have is the sublimation of negative energy into constructive pursuits. Some of the most successful people in the world have this defense mastered, although many are completely unaware of what they are actually doing. Freud's last stage of psychosexual development (genital) spans puberty and adulthood. Like with the phallic stage the focus is on the genitals, but now directed outwards to others as opposed to self-focused. Psychological detachment and independence occurs at this stage. Freud's third essay—The transformations of puberty—examines how puberty and adolescence, corresponding to the genital stage of psychosexual development, consolidates sexuality establishing the dominance of the genitals for sexual gratification. The distinction was made between the "fore-pleasure" of infantile sexuality and the "end-pleasure," meaning pleasure of satisfaction derived from the sexual act.

Beyond the highly complex, and hence unlikely to be accurate nature of Freud's psychosexual theory of development, a major problem is that Freud was too fixated on sexuality. Edward Shorter in his book, A History of Psychiatry, describes how Freud's patient population consisted primarily of young Jewish women. Growing up in middle-class conservative families these young women could not express their sexuality. Psychoanalysis gave them an opportunity to express themselves in this way, and that expression shaped Freud's theories. Shorter believes that if Freud's patient population consisted of lower class Christian women, better able to express their sexuality, his theories would have been much less sexual. Freud's core doctrine was that the trade-off between sexual and aggressive drives, and the demands of reality (reality principle) produces neurotic symptoms. Hence, sexuality had a pivotal role in all mental health issues, extending its influence far beyond sexual behavior itself. Where Freud did seem to have it right and was ahead of his time, as we will see, was in noting that we have a propensity for both types of sexuality, a constitutional bisexuality with each person possessing masculine and feminine tendencies.

Early psychological theories regarding sexual orientation, including those by Freud, tended to link sexual attraction with gender role defined in terms of masculinity/femininity. In other words a man with feminine characteristics providing for a female gender role is drawn to men, while a woman with masculine characteristics representing a male gender role is attracted to females. According to these earlier views heterosexuality is associated with an "appropriate" sex role identity and homosexuality with sex role inversion, meaning characteristics of the other sex including attraction towards one's own sex. Freud believed that an unresolved Oedipal complex caused a young boy to identify with the mother instead of the father, and transform himself into her resulting in sexual attraction towards his own sex. In a similar fashion, an unresolved

Electra complex led to a female taking on a masculine identity with attraction to women.

Research, at least of a more objective nature, reveals that sex role inversion theories are not valid. For example, Michael Storms in his research paper—Theories of sexual orientation—directly tested the notion that homosexual men show lower masculinity and/or higher femininity scores, and homosexual women lower femininity and/or higher masculinity scores, than their heterosexual counterparts. His results indicated that sexual orientation is not related to how masculine or feminine a person is, with no difference emerging between homosexuals, heterosexuals, and bisexuals in regards to femininity and masculinity scores. There is still debate regarding whether or not homosexuals demonstrate more other-sex gender behavior (males feminine and females masculine), and some research such as by Lippa (Sexual orientation and personality) suggests that there is a trend in this direction. However, it appears to be very overstated in most instances based on evidence we will get to shortly. In addition, when a homosexual individual demonstrates pronounced other-sex behavior, mannerisms, and appearance, the real issue might be transgender as covered in the chapter dealing with this intriguing issue.

Storms also tested a theory by Tripp maintaining that homosexuals are strongly attracted to the sex role characteristics of their own sex. Homosexual men are attracted to masculine characteristics to the point of being sexually drawn to men. Tripp indicated that this could occur in both effeminate and masculine men, with the former envying the masculinity they do not have, and the latter identifying with their own masculine nature evidenced in others. According to this theory, homosexual men will show more extremes of masculinity, although there is no speculation of what occurs with homosexual women. Storms found no evidence at all that homosexual men and women show greater variability or extremes on masculine or feminine traits. Tripp's theory also fails to indicate why some men (and presumably women) are excessively drawn to the characteristics of their own sex in the first place.

Psychological theories of sexuality, and certainly those of a psychodynamic nature derived from Freud's early work, emphasize the role of parent-child relationships in sexual orientation. Faulty identification is viewed as the key factor, with the focus more on male homosexuality. A male child is said to identify too closely with women due to the father being absent or rejecting, and/or an overwhelming mother figure. Via the overly close relationship with a female figure the boy acquires feminine behavior leading to a homosexual orientation. For example, Irving Bieber in 1962 (Homosexuality: A Psychoanalytic Study Of Male Homosexuals) argued for a classic homosexual triangle, where the mother is a so-called close binding intimate with the son and is dominating and minimizing towards her husband, who is detached and often hostile detached.

Psychoanalytic studies arose supporting the view that identification with the other-sex parent leads to homosexuality. A British study by O' Connor in 1964 (Aetiological factors in homosexuality as seen in Royal Air Force psychiatric practice) found that 70% of homosexual men were either overly attached to their mothers or distant from their fathers. Braaten and Darling in 1965 reported a study (Overt and covert homosexual problems among male college students) producing results that also supported Bieber's perspective. Comparing homosexual to non-homosexual males, they found that 55% of the former had close binding intimate mothers, compared to only

27

20% of the non-homosexuals. Furthermore, 42% of the homosexuals had detached fathers, compared to only 24% of the non-homosexuals. A 1969 study by Ray Evans (Childhood parental relationships of homosexual men) suggested even greater entanglement of the mother-son relationship—Mothers of homosexual men were described as puritanical, cold towards males, and insisted upon being the center of the son's attention to the point of being seductive. Furthermore, these mothers were said to openly prefer the son over the husband, interfered with the son forming heterosexual romances, discouraged masculine attitudes, and encouraged feminine ones. In regards to the father there was little in the way of a father-son relationship, with the son being fearful of his father and feeling not accepted or respected.

Several other studies by psychoanalysts came to the same basic conclusion that healthy identification with the father failed to occur, typically related to an overly close mother. Faulty identification with the same-sex parent is said to produce homosexuality, via gender role identification with the other-sex parent expressed in masculine and feminine preferences and behaviors, an occurrence that as we have seen is likely inaccurate. In addition to this faulty perspective, these studies were plagued by biases, including statistical errors and reliance on select psychoanalytic patients with conflicts consistent with the theories being investigated. At best there might be a slight trend towards gay males being closer to the mother and distant from the father, but if so this relationship might be a reaction and not a cause. For example, if a son feels different, perhaps derived from attraction to males or effeminate preferences, he might feel alienated from his father, particularly if the father rejects such behavior. The son then becomes closer to the mother in reaction.

Various other social influence theories of homosexuality have been proposed, including homosexual activity or arousal in childhood or adolescence, seduction by an adult of the same sex, being labeled as gay by others, poor peer relationships, a feeling of being different perhaps related to gender behavior, a mother's domination of the father, parental hopes for a child of the other sex, and a parents attitude towards the child, amongst others. To test many of these theories, and also the prominent perspective of identification with the other-sex parent, Bell, Weinberg, and Hammersmith conducted a massive study (Sexual preference: Its development in men and women). An incredible 979 homosexual and 477 heterosexual men and women were assessed using a 528-question structured interview. In the preparation phase they consolidated various hypothesized paths of direct and indirect social influence on adult homosexuality. They eliminated variables and paths that did not differ between homosexuals and heterosexuals until they arrived at a model containing virtually all the hypothesized paths at the time.

The technique that was used by Bell and colleagues is not surprisingly referred to as path analysis. Statistical analysis of the massive amount of data derived from the interviews, indicated how strongly "upstream" variables effected "downstream" variables. For example, how strongly does a mother dominating the father influence childhood gender non-conformity (males displaying feminine behavior, and females masculine behavior), and then how strongly the latter effects adult homosexuality. The so-called path coefficients ranged from .00 to 1.00, with stronger effects indicated by higher numbers, the strongest being 1.00. These researchers concluded that none of the social influence variables hypothesized to cause homosexuality have any merit—Parental relationships or traits, identification with same-sex parent, poor peer relationships, labeling influences, sexual arousal or activity in childhood or adolescence, or seduction by an older same-sex adult. A few examples will help illustrate why they came to this conclusion.

The path coefficient connecting a cold father to a negative relationship with the father was .53, quite low considering how the two would appear tightly linked. The path coefficient between a negative relationship with father and childhood gender non-conformity was much lower at .17, indicating very little relationship. Taking another but related route, the path coefficient from closeness to mother to childhood gender non-conformity was only .14, about the same as the value for a negative relationship with father. Perhaps even more revealing, given the emphasis on other-sex gender behavior, the path coefficient from childhood gender non-conformity to adult homosexuality was a pathetic .12, providing clear evidence that feminine behavior in males and masculine behavior in females does not produce homosexuality in adulthood. Regarding other routes to adult homosexuality, the path from feeling sexually different in childhood to adult homosexuality was only .19, and the path from homosexual activities in adolescence to adult homosexuality a similar .22, both values reflecting very limited influence. The weak path coefficients are evidence against the role of the proposed social influence pathways to adult homosexuality. Furthermore, the very weak path coefficients related to identification with the other-sex parent, basically shoots down psychodynamic formulations of adult homosexuality, and the role of gender non-conformity.

The notion that feminine behavior in males and masculine behavior in females (gender non-conformity) indicates homosexuality tends to persist, most people assuming that an effeminate male is gay and a masculine women lesbian. The results of Bell and colleagues support what I have noted in my own clinical practice, namely that there is no or very little relationship between masculinity/femininity and sexual orientation. I have encountered several very masculine men who identify with being gay, and effeminate men who are heterosexual. Likewise, I have seen women with masculine traits who were "tomboys" in their earlier years showing very strong heterosexual desires, and very traditionally feminine women with a distinct preference for females. Based on my experience as a psychiatrist, I cannot say that there is any real trend regarding gender role behavior aligning tightly with sexual orientation. Some examples will illustrate this reality. One young man I treat for anxiety displays very effeminate mannerisms and speaks in a very soft voice with a lisp. His body build is muscular and fit, with clean facial features. The vast majority of people would place him as being gay based on his effeminate mannerisms and speech. However, he is straight with no apparent desire for males and has never experienced gay sex. His wife who attended a few sessions indicated that he is very robust sexually. A middle-aged man I see for depression is model thin and extremely neat, with perfectly groomed hair even in stormy weather. He wears bold "effeminate" colors such as pink and yellow. His speech and mannerisms tend to be a mix of masculine and feminine. Although the verdict would not be as unanimous as in the first example, a sizeable number of people would suspect he is gay based on his more effeminate dress, body build, and style. Once again he is straight, married, with no gay sexual experiences.

Another middle-age man is tall, strong, and rough in his mannerisms, such as the way he walks and gestures. His speech is powerful and he often comes across as somewhat aggressive. In regards to dress and style he wears old well-worn casual shoes and clothes, and his hair is often disheveled. Consistent with his masculine appearance, mannerisms, speech, and dress, he works in a very "masculine" occupation and loves the work. Based on the suspected association of masculinity and heterosexuality, virtually everyone would agree he is straight. They would be wrong though as he identifies with being gay, only trying a few heterosexual relationships early in his teenage years and partaking in gay sex throughout his life. Another man I treat for anxiety is overweight with no apparent concern for his physical appearance. His mannerisms are mostly masculine, and his preferences are for beer and barbeques more than "effeminate" things. He is also gay despite his "masculine" nature.

The same applies to females that I have seen in my clinical practice. One very stylish woman highly concerned about her weight, figure, dress, and hairstyle, identifies as being mostly lesbian, although she can partake in sex with the occasional man. I have encountered other so-called "lipstick" lesbians that based on their feminine appearance and mannerisms would never be pegged as being gay. Meanwhile, one fairly young woman I treat for depression is overweight, stocky, rarely bothers fixing her hair even when feeling good, shows masculine mannerisms such as with gestures and swearing. She is married and greatly enjoys sex with her husband, as she did with other men prior to marriage. Having treated numerous men and women over many years, with them sharing very personal information regarding their sexual orientation given the nature of psychiatric treatment, I simply do not see any clear association between masculinity/femininity and sexual orientation.

What about the possibility of other psychological forces influencing sexual orientation and sexuality? An alternative to psychoanalysis is behaviorism arguing that all behaviors are shaped by reinforcement. Reinforcement increases the frequency of a behavior, whereas punishment reduces it. If a given behavior leads to a positive outcome the behavior is positively reinforced. For example, as a male you act in an effeminate fashion and your friends praise you for it. Negative reinforcement occurs when an action reduces or eliminates negative circumstances. For instance, you incur hostility from those around you until you start to act effeminate. A behavioral perspective on sexuality indicates that masculinity/femininity and sexual orientation result from reinforcement and even punishment effects. Hence, if you are "gay" it is because the environment has reinforced that type of behavior or punished the alternative. The study by Bell and colleagues disproves this notion, given that some of the paths they investigated relate to environmental reinforcement and punishment. For example, the path from a strong mother to homosexual activities in childhood revealed a path coefficient of only .11, a very low value considering the potential reinforcing effects of a powerful mother on sexual behavior. Even more revealing is the low path coefficient of .21 from homosexual genital activities in childhood to homosexual activities in adolescence. The presence of such activity in childhood with the sexual pleasure it brings (recall how children are quite sexual), would seemingly reinforce such behavior making it common a few years later in adolescence.

None of the results found by Bell and colleagues support a behavioral explanation any more than they do a psychodynamic perspective. Even at face value it seems unlikely that environmental reinforcement could produce sexual preferences, such as masculine and feminine behavior or sexual orientation, unless there was some underlying propensity for it in the first place. Also relevant is the question of why an individual would try a given behavior in the first place. Behaviorist might argue that it just occurs and reinforcement effects determine whether or not it will increase or decrease in frequency. However, it is more likely that something within the person motivates the behavior in the first place, and then the environment might or might not have an impact. So far it seems as if psychological theories of sexuality are a complete washout, but there are key influences that actually do play a prominent role. They consist of sexual dimension activation, erotic fantasy, and social construction, topics we will explore in other chapters.

BIOLOGICAL THEORIES

Given that sex ultimately is biologically based, is it is not at all surprising that sexual orientation, and sexuality more generally, has been attributed to biological causation. Numerous explanations of this type, many very complex in nature, have been proposed throughout the history of research pertaining to sexual orientation, and only the more significant ones will be covered here. Although highly intertwined, I will divide these theories into hormonal, brain-based, genetic, evolutionary, and miscellaneous. There is definite overlap among or between these and one often follows from the other, such as with brain changes arising from hormonal differences.

HORMONAL EXPLANATIONS:

Animal experiments in the last half of the 20th century, suggested that exposure to male hormones (androgens) prior to birth in the intrauterine environment (prenatally), result in masculinization of the genitals and brain. Androgens such as testosterone were discovered in 1936, and are the hormones responsible for the development of male characteristics. It was found that when a mother rat is injected with male sex hormones, female offspring developed masculinized external genitalia and displayed more male typical sexual behavior. The rat brain is basically female and requires male hormones to grow into the male pattern. Therefore, if rats are exposed to excess androgens early on in the intrauterine environment they are masculinized, and if exposed to low levels of androgens early on are feminized.

Female rats exposed to high levels of androgens later in prenatal development, exhibit increased aggression and sexual activity directed towards females, such as mounting them. Male rats exposed to low levels of androgens later in prenatal development, demonstrate more sexually submissive behavior, such as being mounted by male rats.

Extrapolating from rats to humans is difficult, despite some people being accused of acting like rats, because sexuality in rats, although complex, is vastly more straightforward. For humans it is not simply a matter of mounting or being mounted, and the range of behaviors related to sexuality and sexual orientation is enormous. However, prenatal androgens appear to play a role in masculine/feminine behavior and hence core gender identity (a person's sense of being male or female). Female hormones (estrogens) seem to have much less of an impact on these important aspects of sexuality. For many or most animal species, not just rats, sexual behavior differing between the sexes is guided by hormonal influences on brain structures pre or perinatally (around the time of birth), with higher androgen levels during sensitive periods contributing to masculine behavior and lesser levels feminine behavior as described by Gooren and Kruijver (Androgens and male behavior).

In humans high levels of androgens such as from drug treatment or a condition known as congenital adrenal hyperplasia, result in masculine tomboyish behavior in girls, as indicated by Hines (Prenatal testosterone and gender-related behaviour). However, the impact on sexual orientation appears to be very limited or negligible. Any influence of male hormones on sexual orientation, beyond the indirect effect via masculine/feminine behavior and gender identity, might even be via increased thrill-seeking—James proposed

36

(Biological and psychosocial determinants of male and female human sexual orientation) that higher androgen levels might encourage more thrill seeking, expressed at least partly in the form of homosexual behavior. Despite years of research, no clear and reproducible findings suggesting an appreciable impact of sex hormones on sexual orientation, at least as we commonly understand it, have emerged.

BRAIN-BASED STRUCTURES:

The main region of the brain that has been implicated in sexual orientation is the hypothalamus, a key structure in the regulation of sexual behavior. Dorner proposed in 1988 that underexposure of male brains to prenatal androgens results in female differentiation of the hypothalamus in male homosexuals. The preoptic area of the hypothalamus when damaged in male animals was known to reduce interest in mating with females. Swaab and Fliess in 1985 located a nucleus within the preoptic area that appears to be larger in males, that they named the sexually dimorphic nucleus (SDN). A four-nuclei group of the preoptic area came to be known as the interstitial nuclei of the anterior hypothalamus, a real mouth full, abbreviated as INAH and numbered 1-4, with the SDN known as INAH-1.

A milestone study by Simon LeVay occurred in 1991 (A difference in hypothalamic structure between heterosexual and homosexual men), whereby INAH 1-4 were examined in the brains of 19 homosexual men who died of Acquired Immune Deficiency Syndrome (AIDS), 16 men who were presumed to be heterosexual, and 6 women that were supposedly heterosexual. LeVay did not find any difference between the three subject groups for INAH-1, INAH-2, INAH-4, but did find that INAH-3 was half the size in the homosexual men compared to the presumably heterosexual men, and the same size as those of the heterosexual women. This suggested that a brain structure—the INAH-3 nucleus of the preoptic area of the hypothalamus—is linked to sexual orientation. Life would be so simple if sexual orientation depended on the size of a nucleus in the hypothalamus, but rarely can complex behaviors such as sexual orientation in humans be reduced to such a simplistic level. Consistent with this notion, there have been numerous critiques of LeVay's results. A major issue is that the homosexual subjects died of AIDS, and hence the INAH-3 results could have been due to the disease and not being homosexual. However, when the 6 heterosexual men who died of AIDS (likely due to blood transfusions) were compared to the homosexual group the results held.

A further problem with LeVay's results was that 3 of the heterosexuals had smaller INAH-3 nuclei than the homosexuals, and 3 of the homosexuals had larger INAH-3 nuclei than did the heterosexuals. LeVay acknowledged that these exceptions ensured that INAH-3 size alone does not determine human sexual orientation. He also indicated that the correlational nature of the results do not prove causation; in other words the smaller INAH-3 size in the homosexuals could have resulted from this sexual orientation, or the HIV virus causing AIDS, and not been the cause of homosexual orientation. Follow-up studies have tended not to support LeVay's results. This is a common occurrence in the field of neuroscience, and perhaps science more generally, with initial results not holding out to further investigations. William Byne and colleagues repeated the study in 2001 (The interstitial nuclei of the anterior hypothalamus: An investigation of variance with sex, sexual orientation, and HIV status) with 14 HIV positive homosexual men, 34 presumably heterosexual men (10 HIV positive), and 34 supposedly heterosexual women (9 HIV positive). They did not find any statistically significant difference in the size of the INAH-3 nucleus between the three groups, although there was a trend for homosexual men to have smaller size than heterosexual men, and larger size than heterosexual women. However, research is based on statistical significance and trends do not count. They also weighed and counted the number of neurons in INAH-3, but once again there were no statistically significant differences between the three groups.

The search for brain regions differing between gay and straight people has not stopped at the INAH nuclei of the hypothalamus. Additional structures examined include the suprachiasmatic nucleus (SCN) of the hypothalamus, and the anterior commissure (AC) amongst others. Swaab and colleagues found that the suprachiasmatic nucleus of the hypothalamus was larger and contained more cells in heterosexual men compared to homosexual men. Their results have been criticized based upon the SCN not varying in size between the sexes, and hence not being relevant to sexual orientation. Swaab and colleagues themselves have critiqued the INAH results mentioned above and their relationship to prenatal androgen levels, by indicating that although sex hormones peak in the second half of gestation, there is no difference in the so-called sexually dimorphic nucleus, and no fetal brain receptors for sex hormones present at this point. A reasonable way of summarizing results for hypothalamic nuclei is that, although biological influences on sex is clearly a complex matter and there is never-ending debate, the results do not seem to support much of a role for these nuclei in sexual orientation.

The anterior commissure (AC) is one of the structures connecting the two hemispheres of the brain.

39

Allen and Gorski in 1992 (Sexual orientation and the size of the anterior commissure in the human brain) reported that this structure is 34% larger in homosexual men than heterosexual men. Given that this structure, like the suprachiasmatic nucleus, does not seem to play a role in sexuality, it appears unlikely that it would differ with sexual orientation. Mitchell Lasco and colleagues (A lack of dimorphism of sex or sexual orientation in the human anterior commissure) did a follow-up study in 2002 examining the brains of 120 individuals. They found no difference in the size of the AC based on, age, HIV status, sex, or sexual orientation. In addition, even if Allen and Gorski's findings could be replicated, there is so much overlap in AC size between homosexual and heterosexual men that the results would be meaningless. Hence, much like the results for the INAH nuclei and SCN of the hypothalamus, there does not appear to be any real validity to purported differences in the AC with sexual orientation.   Over time despite many attempts, no brain structure has been shown to reliably vary with sexual orientation.

GENETIC:

Genes code not only for biological structures, but for behaviors as well. At a very rudimentary level the beating of your heart and breathing represent behaviors that are genetically encoded. At a more conscious level feeding and sexual behaviors have their basis in our genetic material, such as young children putting everything in their mouth to see if it is edible, and male erections in response to sexual stimuli. Hence, the notion that sexual orientation and other aspects of human sexuality have a genetic basis is logical. Twins offer a

40

fantastic way to assess genetic influences on behavior. Identical or monozygotic twins are born from the same egg that divides, meaning that they share 100% of their genes. Fraternal or dizygotic twins come from two separate eggs, but are born at the same time. Given that fraternal twins come from two separate eggs they share far fewer genes than identical twins. Hence, by comparing the frequency of a behavior between identical and fraternal twins, researchers can get an idea of how genetic a behavior is. However, what about shared environmental influences greater with identical twins given that they are the same sex and look the same? Parents and others will treat them almost as if they are the same person. For that reason the ideal in twin research is to find identical and fraternal twins reared apart in different families, where there can be no shared environmental influence, at least beyond the womb. Any variation in the frequency of a trait occurring between identical and fraternal twins must then arise from genes (or influences in the womb).

Finding identical and fraternal twins reared apart is not easy, and most studies examining the influence of genes on sexual orientation involve comparisons between identical and fraternal twins, as well as adopted siblings sharing no genes at all, raised in the same family. A seminal study was undertaken by Bailey and Pillard in 1991 (A genetic study of male sexual orientation) to compare identical and fraternal twins. Responding to criticisms of prior research they recruited from homosexual publications. This step was taken because earlier genetic studies sampled from institutions, raising the possibility of a highly restricted and hence biased sample. Bailey and Pillard also made a solid effort to accurately rate zygosity (identical or fraternal) and sexual orientation by employing detailed questionnaires. Their results indicated that identical twins are 52% concordant for homosexuality and bisexuality, compared to 22% for fraternal twins and 11% for adopted brothers. Clearly sharing 100% of genes translates into a much greater likelihood that siblings will be similar in sexual orientation. Interestingly, despite identical genes and similar shared environment, approximately 50% did not end up having the same sexual orientation, meaning that forces other than genes and shared environmental influences must also play a major role.

As some of you might well be realizing at this point, biological research pertaining to sexual orientation is overwhelmingly focused on males, with little attention paid to females. Bailey and colleagues in 1993 (Heritable factors influence sexual orientation in women) assessed female homosexuals using a similar methodology to the 1991 study. They found concordance rates consistent with their findings for male homosexuals—48% for monozygotic twins, 22% for dizygotic twins, and 6% for adoptive sisters. It turns out though that bias in these studies prevents us from accepting the figures as being fully valid. There are several problems one being that the ideal of twins reared apart from each other was not used. Another problem is that the degree of zygosity and sexual orientation was based on reports. Only one twin of a pair was interviewed and asked to give information pertaining to whether or not the other is an identical twin, and of what sexual orientation. To overcome these problems data from twin registries is required. In different parts of the world twins are registered with detailed information regarding their medical history, including whether or not they are identical or fraternal. In 2000 Bailey and colleagues published a study (Genetic and environmental influences on sexual orientation and its correlates in an Australian twin sample) using a twin registry. A concordance rate of 20% was found for identical male twins and 24% for identical female twins, substantially lower than the 50% figures obtained with the other methodology.

Due to methodological limitations and uncertainties with twin studies another technique known as genetic linkage has been employed. To make a long and complex story short and simple, a trait is isolated in an extended family and genes "linked" to this trait are searched for. In 1993 Dean Hamer and colleagues (A linkage between DNA markers on the X-chromosome and male sexual orientation) published a study assessing 114 families of homosexual males for genetic linkages. They found that the homosexual males in their sample had more homosexual uncles and cousins on the maternal side of the family than on the paternal side. This occurrence suggested that male homosexuality might arise from genes on the X chromosome inherited from the mother— Males are XY, with the Y coming from the father making them male; females are XX, with one X chromosome from the mother and one from the father. They then tested 40 male sibling pairs and found similar alleles (versions of the same gene) in the q28 region of the X chromosome in 33, well above the expected rate of 20/40. Media seized on the results and q28 was dubbed the "gay gene." Politics entered the arena with some gay advocates supporting the finding given that if male homosexuality is strictly genetic it has to be normal. On the other side, opponents suggested that this was proof that homosexuality was a defect based on genes.

Throughout the history of genetic research there has been a tendency to try and find single genes responsible for complex physical and behavioral entities, but the reality is that most complex biological events involve the interaction of multiple genes and the environment, with the latter even playing a role in turning

43

genes on and off. Hence, one gene accounting for male homosexual orientation is highly unlikely. Dean Hamer and colleagues did not suggest that they had found the "gay gene," and were much more cautious in interpreting their own results. They even indicated that if the genetics of male homosexuality were like those for eye color based on a single gene (Mendelian), the rate of homosexual orientation in maternal uncles and cousins would be far higher. They also indicated that there were instances in their sample of gay relatives on the father's side. These researchers were content with suggesting that Xq28 might be one genetic contributor to a homosexual orientation. This belief might even be overly optimistic based on an interesting comment by Miron Baron in 1993 (Genetic linkage and male homosexual orientation). Baron indicated that at one point bipolar disorder (manic-depressive illness) was linked to Xq27-28, and more strongly than for male homosexuality, but the results did not hold up to further investigations. In 1999 Rice and colleagues attempted to replicate Hamer's findings for Xq28 using 52 gay male sibling pairs (Male homosexuality: Absence of linkage to microsatellite markers at xq28). As the title suggests, they did not find any linkage to this site.

The results of the study by Rice in 1999 were backed up by a more extensive study by Mustanski and colleagues in 2005 (A genome wide scan of male sexual orientation). These researchers did the first genome wide scan of male homosexuality using a sample of 456 individuals from 146 unrelated families. There had to be exclusive maternal transmission (gay relatives on the mother's side only) and at least two gay brothers. Xq28 did not emerge as a significant site, but three others on chromosomes 7 (q36), 8 (p12), and 10 (q26) did. 7q36 had the strongest linkage with equivalent maternal and paternal transmission. 8p12 showed weaker results, but like 7q36 revealed both maternal and paternal transmission. 10q26 demonstrated the weakest linkage of the three, and only maternal transmission. Unfortunately from the perspective of finding genetic linkages, theses results fall below the standard criteria for genome wide significance, with only 7q36 coming close. There are additional genetic linkage studies but none has shown anything definitive and strongly replicable, suggesting that at most various genes might contribute to a homosexual orientation with each providing only a small influence.

EVOLUTIONARY:

Natural selection as advanced in the mid 19th century by Charles Darwin, indicates that traits increasing the bearer's success at surviving and reproducing become more represented in subsequent generations. Darwin did not have the luxury of knowing about actual genes, but worked out his powerful theory on the basis of trait observations. Homosexuality appears to produce an evolutionary or Darwinian paradox, because genes working against reproduction should theoretically vanish from the gene pool. However, as some theorists have suggested there might be indirect ways that being homosexual can facilitate the success of the genes you have. In this regard there are four main perspectives consisting of kin selection, male heterozygous advantage, balanced polymorphism, and sexual antagonism.

Kin selection occurs when your own genes are passed on via relatives. Even though you might not survive and reproduce, if family members sharing many of your genes do, then your genes also demonstrate evolutionary fitness. To take an obvious example, you rescue your siblings from a lake preventing them from drowning, but you die in the process. Even though you are no longer around to reproduce and propagate your own genes, your siblings sharing many of your own genes pass them on to succeeding generations. In 1978 E.O. Wilson proposed in his book, On Human Nature, that homosexuals help those who share their genes, such as family members, thereby facilitating the passage of their own genes despite an absence of reproductive behavior. This theory presumes that homosexual individuals are more altruistic, at least to kin, but there is no evidence that homosexuals are more altruistic, as Small demonstrates in his 1995 book, What's Love Got To Do With It? The Evolution Of Human Mating. Even thinking of homosexual individuals you know, it would be difficult to claim that these individuals are clearly more altruistic than non-gay acquaintances. Some even have little or nothing to do with their families, and certainly not more on average than non-homosexual people. Animals showing homosexual behavior seem to provide more support to their partners than kin, in contrast to what is predicted by Wilson's kin selection hypothesis. For example, Yamagiwa studying mountain gorillas, Akers and Conway reporting on macaque monkeys, and Parish examining chimpanzees, found that homosexual behavioral pairings provided more resources to the partner than to relatives. Hence, it is safe to say that kin selection does not account for homosexual behavior.

The second theory—male heterozygous advantage—as expressed by MacIntyre and Estep in 1993, and Hutchinson back in 1959, states that in a mixed form consisting of both a homosexual and heterosexual gene there might be an advantage. A heterozygous advantage is seen in very select instances, such as in the case of sickle cell anemia where one copy of the sickle cell gene (heterozygous) provides protection from malaria, but with two copies (homozygous) potentially fatal anemia (reduced capacity of the blood cells to carry oxygen) can occur. Individuals lacking a single sickle cell gene are more vulnerable to malaria. Given the much higher preponderance of malaria in tropical countries, sickle cell genes are found almost exclusively in dark skinned people. In a similar fashion, one copy of the homosexual gene might provide an advantage of some sort, such as perhaps greater nurturing behavior, without actual homosexuality. Two copies though produce homosexual behavior seen as being flawed. A fatal flaw of this theory is that complex behaviors, such as sexual orientation, do not work by a single gene mechanism as occurs with sickle cell anemia or eye color.

An explanation that incorporates the notion of multiple genes influencing sexual orientation is that of so-called balanced polymorphism, the poly referring to multiple genes. The notion here as expressed by Miller in 2008 (Homosexuality, birth order, and evolution: Toward an equilibrium reproductive economics of homosexuality) is that feminizing alleles make a man a better father and more attractive mate, thereby enhancing evolutionary fitness, while at the same time promoting homosexuality. In a balanced state there is an advantage, but if too many feminizing genes occur, then the man becomes homosexual reducing reproductive success. This theory is vastly flawed in several ways, one being the repeated notion that homosexual men are more effeminate, a perspective that is not able to explain why many homosexual men are very masculine, and even more intensely than many heterosexual men.

Another major flaw is that it perpetuates the widespread notion that men are useless to childrearing, aside from sperm and a paycheck as is often noted, unless they have feminine qualities. This is a gross degrading of the role of fathers in childrearing, and a view that is only now undergoing some shifting from the centuries long dark ages. Enlightened research is emerging that fathers with normal masculine traits actually do play an important role in the wellbeing of their children. For example, Tither and Ellis (Impact of father's on daughters' age at menarche: A genetically and environmentally controlled sibling study) discovered that teenage daughters having an emotional connection to their father (and not one based on feminine qualities) actually experience a biologically based delay of puberty onset, and reduced propensity to become pregnant in their teens! The notion being that without the security of a father in place, the reproductive system takes a quicker and faster strategy, given that waiting might not be an option. On the other hand, the security of a protective father allows for a strategy of slower and healthier maturation of the reproductive system and delayed childbearing. Evidence for the biological basis comes from the finding that the delayed reproductive strategy is activated largely by the smell of the father communicated by pheromones (a secreted or excreted chemical factor that triggers a social response in members of the same species). Other notions of the balanced polymorphism theory can be called into question, such as that women are truly sexually attracted to men with feminine qualities, a highly dubious proposition.

The fourth major evolutionary theory of homosexuality—sexually antagonistic selection—is based on the work of Andrea Ciani, Paolo Cermelli, and Giovanni Zanzotto: Sexually antagonistic selection in human male homosexuality. These researchers noted four points pertaining to male homosexuality—It occurs at a stable frequency in many populations, female relatives of gay men produce children at a higher rate than other women, amongst these female relatives those related to the gay man's mother reproduce at a higher rate than those related to his father, and homosexuality is more common in male relatives related to the gay man's mother than father. The argument goes that, although the gay males reproduction suffers, the reproductive success of his female relatives possessing the same genetic material increases. Their study applies complex mathematical analysis to various potential models that might account for these occurrences, and concludes that the only valid one is sexual antagonism benefiting female relatives reproduction, at the expense of males having a homosexual genetic constitution.

The theory of sexually antagonistic selection applied to homosexuality has many problems associated with it. To start it can only account for male sexuality and has nothing to say about female homosexuality. In all likelihood, at least from the perspective of the simplest and most parsimonious explanation being the most accurate, the origins of male and female homosexuality must share substantial commonality. Given that the sexual antagonism theory is highly complex and non-parsimonious, it is not likely to stand the test of time. Relevant to the complexity of the sexual antagonism theory of male homosexuality, it is based on some dubious assumptions that are unlikely to hold across the entire spectrum of homosexual males, one being that homosexuality is more common in male relatives on the mother's side than the father's side. As we learned from the study by Mutansky and colleagues, two of the three genes linked to male homosexuality were derived from both maternal and paternal transmission. Furthermore, there does not appear to be solid evidence that male homosexuals are more common on the mother's side. In quite a number of instances I have observed high rates of homosexuality on the paternal side of my psychiatric patients, with the behavior being hidden in some cases. For example, a 50-year old man with depression has 3 sons, two gay. Upon coming to trust me he disclosed that he was predominately gay. A key reason for his depressed state was that he could not "come out" to anyone he knew, keeping him forever isolated in the proverbial closet. This man spent 3 months in a psychiatric hospital only improving slightly despite medication, because he could not trust anyone enough in that setting to reveal the core problem. Another man openly gay has two gay brothers (of three total), and although his father is apparently straight, there are some male relatives on his father's side who never married and seemed to be "perpetual bachelors."

There is some support for sexual antagonism in limited populations, amongst either or both, the female and male lines. For example, Vanderlaan and colleagues found increased "reproductive output" for grandmothers, but not aunts and uncles, on both the female and male sides of homosexual men (fa'afafine) in Samoa. For this theory to be valid "reproductive output" should be enhanced amongst various female relatives of homosexual men, not just specific ones such as grandmothers. The other assumptions of Ciani and colleagues—female relatives of a homosexual man's mother reproduce at a higher rate than those related to his father, and homosexuality is more common in male relatives related to the gay man's mother than father—appear to be ones that will not stand up well to repeated sampling of different populations, conducted by researchers not invested in the sexual antagonism theory. We must then conclude that evolutionary theories attempting to explain the evolutionary paradox are completely false or at best weak and restricted to male homosexuality.

MISCELLANEOUS:

Many weird and wonderful biological perspectives on sexual orientation have been proposed. Some view homosexuality as an innate biologically based state. The German lawyer Karl-Heinrich Ulrichs from 1864 to 1879 published a series of pamphlets declaring "man-male love" to be inborn. This love resulted from the natural and healthy expression of a female soul in a male body, a condition he called Uranism. Given how natural this condition is "Uranians" as he called them should not be legally persecuted. Indeed a very enlightened legal view, and one orientated to reducing the suffering of homosexual men. Encompassing female homosexuals in his theory, something quite rare even today, Magnus Hirschfeld in 1896 published in a German pamphlet "Sappho and Socrates," a theory proposing that the origin of homosexuality resides in a bisexual embryo. He postulated the existence of rudimentary neural centers for attraction to both males and females in the embryos of both sexes. In most female fetuses the center for attraction to men developed while the center for attraction to women receded, the reverse occurring in men. Homosexuality was postulated to arise from the center for same-sex attraction developing and the center for opposite sex attraction receding. In many ways Hirshfeld was ahead of his time, as we will see later on by postulating distinct brain based same-sex and other-sex attractions, although there does not appear to be actual centers.

A more bizarre theory with dangerous consequences was that of Eugen Steinbach who described (1917) in Jarbuch fur sextuelle Zwischenstufen (Yearbook of Sexual Intermediaries) his research results of transplanting testes and ovaries in rats and guinea pigs. He indicated that these glands produce hormones that enter into the bloodstream and produce both physical and sexual characteristics, a very accurate observation. The secretions were said to be responsible for the sexualization of the brain as male or female, a process occurring early in life based on how the transplantations were far more effective when performed shortly after birth. So far this sounds very scientific and solid, but then Steinbach takes a very interesting detour, proposing that testicular secretions in homosexual men are abnormal and drive brain development in a female direction. He claimed to see microscopic differences in the structure of the testes between homosexual and heterosexual men, particularly in terms of the interstitial cells responsible for testicular secretions. He transplanted a testicle from a heterosexual man into an "effeminate and passive" homosexual man, claiming that the man was totally cured, losing attraction to men and developing heterosexual desires. Further successes were reported by him, but later shown to be ineffective. We can only wonder who in their right or wrong mind would donate a testicle for such an experiment!

Moving ahead to more recent times an expanding literature associates male "homosexuality" with a fraternal birth order effect and handedness. Ray Blanchard, based on a sample of gay men, noted that males with older brothers are more likely to be gay. Additional studies have found a trend in this direction. To account for this occurrence, Blanchard proposed a maternal immune hypothesis stating that male specific antigens increase in the mother with exposure to more male fetuses. During delivery the mother's body becomes exposed to male antigens, and the immune system reacts producing antibodies against these antigens. The first-born male escapes free and clear, but subsequent male offspring are exposed to these antibodies, that presumably increase with each male child and promote homosexuality. Hence, the probability of being homosexual increases with each male sibling. A major problem with this theory is that most homosexual males lack siblings, have only sisters, or are the oldest of the male siblings. How possibly can these occurrences be reconciled with an immune attack hypothesis of homosexuality? At best it might account for a small percentage of male homosexuality. In addition, since female specific antibodies cannot arise with female offspring, given that the mother is also female, the theory or proposed mechanism cannot remotely explain female homosexuality. However, Vaderlaan and colleagues, one being Blanchard, have found that homosexual females have an excess of sisters.

Complicating the theory further, non-right-handedness apparently increases the chances of a man being gay, except in the scenario where he is the youngest of several male children, and then the fraternal birth order effect is eliminated, according to Blanchard. This requires some very convoluted explaining, as Valenzuela attempted suggesting that somehow non-right-handedness induces tolerance of mothers for "anti-female factors," or changes the maternal compatibility of "gay" embryos. From a statistical perspective, the "a priori" probability (prior to a study being conducted) of a result being true influences the interpretation of a positive research outcome—If the a priori probability of a result being true is high the outcome is meaningful, but if the a priori probability is low then a positive outcome only measures bias involved in achieving the positive outcome. This major statistical issue actually means that most research finding are false, according to John Ionnides in his paper, Why most published research findings are false. By any reasonable standard, the a prior probability of the fraternal birth order effect and handedness outcomes being true must be extremely low, rendering these outcomes a measure of bias, such as with sampling. In support of this conjecture, Bearman and Bruckner (Opposite-sex twins and adolescent same-sex attraction) did not find any association between same-sex attraction and number of older siblings, and argue that non-representative samples and/or indirect reports on siblings' sexual orientation are present in studies finding a fraternal birth order effect.

Regarding the male antibody explanation for the fraternal birth order effect, Whitehead (An antiboy antibody? Re-examination of the maternal immune hypothesis) found that the immune system mechanism proposed by Blanchard lacks validity. One problem with the proposed mechanism is that the immune system is highly efficient, and one exposure typically is all that is required to produce an effective antibody response. Based on this reality the male specific antibody response should be approximately the same far all male offspring after the first one, resulting in no homosexuality in the first-born and the same frequency in all additional male offspring, not increased frequency with each older brother. Further working against the male antibody concept is the finding by Kangassalo and colleagues in a Finnish sample, indicating that non-heterosexual men not only have more older brothers, but more older sisters than heterosexual men. Clearly the male antibody mechanism cannot account for this finding.

54

SUMMARY OF BIOLOGICAL THEORIES:

There are no shortage of biological explanations for male homosexuality, and at least some for female homosexuality. It does appear that male hormones can influence masculine and feminine behavior, and hence, core gender identity. However, the impact of male (and female) hormones on sexual orientation is negligible or non-existent. As we learned in the psychological theory chapter, masculinity/femininity might at most have a weak impact on sexual orientation, despite widespread beliefs to the contrary. Hence, even if hormones influence masculinity/femininity the effect on sexual orientation is still not significant. Although it might seem logical that sexual orientation be derived from brain structures, research has not supported this perspective, and no truly replicable findings have emerged. Despite the excitement over the possibility of a "gay gene," genetics research does not support a single gene, and at best multiple genes from both the mothers and fathers side play some role, although perhaps a limited one.

Evolutionary explanations such as kin selection, male heterozygous advantage, balanced polymorphism, and sexual antagonism, appear to be based on flawed assumptions, and/or biased sampling, rendering them largely invalid. While entertaining, the miscellaneous explanations also fail to provide a solid biological rationale. These poor results do not mean that there is no biological basis at all to sexual orientation, and considering how prominent such behavior is it is a safe bet that there must be some biological basis. The answer though turns out to be much different from what researchers have considered, largely because they all have assumed that "homosexuality" and "heterosexuality," in and of themselves, are real entities. It is amazing that not one of these biological researchers or theorists has pulled back and asked whether these sexual orientation categories might just be partially accurate descriptions of natural occurring events! If it is the case that they are not real entities, then explanations based on this premise are severely flawed from the start. As we will see shortly, there is another way to approach sexual orientation, not embedded in the assumption that homosexuality and heterosexuality are true entities. The answer explains both male and female homosexuality, making it a much more parsimonious perspective than theories only capable of accounting for homosexuality in one sex.

ANIMAL "HOMOSEXUALITY"

People are typically quite surprised to learn that homosexual behavior is present in animals, commonly believing that it is unique to us humans. I will use the term homoerotic and heteroerotic behavior when discussing animal sexuality to get away from any connotations implied by the term "homosexuality." Certain interesting themes worth highlighting emerge when looking at sexual research focused on animals. Perhaps the foremost one is that unbiased observation tends to uncover more homoerotic behavior. As with any behavior homoerotic actions take time and unbiased observing to detect. For example, let's assume that you are from another planet and have been sent to record sexuality in humans. Your species prefers heteroerotic behavior with homoerotic behavior being somewhat frowned upon. Once on the planet Earth you start observing and note male and female couples holding hands, embracing, and kissing. You go to a movie theatre to learn even more about human sexuality, and see male-female couples making love on screen.

Noticing movement and an odd sound in the back row of the theatre, you turn and observe a young man and woman engaging in sexual play. It seems obvious that humans as a species are heterosexual based on your observations to this point. Then you notice two females a few rows up engage in what appears to be sexual behavior, with one putting her arm around the other. Believing that humans are heterosexual much as is your species, you decide that one person was comforting the other. However, being a dedicated researcher you decide

57

to investigate further, and start looking in bedroom windows at night to see what is really going on. Of course you have to be careful, because it would not do for you to be caught and it be revealed that an alien was observing us humans. To your amazement you discover that men are having sex with men, and women with women. The decision to investigate further was crucial to this discovery, as was your willingness to believe what you are seeing and report it as such.

Early observations of animals in the wild were biased in favor of seeing heteroerotic behavior, based on how unacceptable it was to report the alternative. There are even cases where a researcher would observe homoerotic behavior and offer the research material to another investigator, out of fear that his or her career would suffer if the material was published. Unfortunately, the goal of research for many academics, both back then and now, is to advance careers. Fortunately, though, the truth ultimately prevails because the foremost goal of scientific research is to yield true outcomes. With unbiased observation and reporting it has become very clear that animal homoerotic behavior is extremely common. A second key theme from this research is that such behavior occurs in diverse species including insects, reptiles, fish, birds, mammals, and primates. According to Bruce Bagemihl, the author of the 1999 book Biological Exuberance: Animal Homosexuality and Natural Diversity, such behavior has been observed in 1,500 distinct species and well documented in 500 of these! Indeed it seems that homoerotic behavior is feasible in virtually every species with distinct sexes.

Bagemihl looked at research extending back into the 1700's and was shocked by what he encountered, not so much as pertains to animal sexuality, but in regards to how the subject was treated by early researchers. He

58

noted that if the gender of animals engaged in sexual behavior could not be determined, it was assumed they were other-sex. In several instances homosexuality was discounted as unnatural, aberrant, and even outright deviant. Various explanations designed to rationalize it were suggested, such as oral-genital behavior serving a nutritional function, or only practice for real heterosexual encounters. Another common rationalization was that captive animals engage in homosexual acts due to confinement, implying that such behavior is not at all natural. It is now known that homoerotic behavior is very natural in the wild. The social norms and morals of the time strongly influenced the perspectives of these early researchers, or at the very least guided what they put into print.

A major reason why homoerotic behavior was not widely reported early on relates to a third theme in animal sexuality research, that being a fixation on the reproductive function of sex. If it is assumed that the function of sex is strictly for reproduction, then you as a researcher have to discover how the observed behavior facilitates reproduction. In the case of heterorotic behavior this is quite straightforward, but much more of a challenge when it comes to homoerotic behavior. The mindset that sexual behavior exists solely for reproduction is arguably one of the most graphic examples of researchers being stymied by a fixated perspective. If homoerotic behavior is observed then the reproductive value has to be ascertained. This fixated perspective aligns with the evolutionary or Darwinian paradox of attempting to explain how behavior that seemingly detracts from reproduction could have evolved. Few considered that sexual behavior might have multiple functions, most not directly, or even necessarily indirectly, related to reproduction. As we cover examples of animal homoerotic behavior we will see that there are many viable functions beyond reproduction. The examples provided will also reveal a fourth major theme—While there are countless instances of homoerotic behavior in diverse animal species, there are very few examples of exclusive homosexual orientation. Nature does not appear to favor an actual orientation to homoerotic or heteroerotic behavior, an occurrence with profound implications for human sexuality as we will get to. A fifth theme is that as cognitive sophistication or intelligence increases, so does the complexity of homoerotic behavior. In insects such behavior is quite stereotyped and rigid, but very creative and diverse in mammals, such as dolphins, and also primates, us humans included.

EXAMPLES OF HOMOEROTIC BEHAVIOR IN ANIMALS:

As we examine homoerotic behavior in animals, proposed functions of this behavior will be highlighted to reveal how sexual behavior has many benefits. Hopefully, this information will free your mind from the perspective that has trapped so many researchers—Sex strictly for reproduction. With an open mind many things are possible including an acceptance of homoerotic behavior in humans as completely natural, and not something to discriminate against. I will start with more cognitively simple organisms and proceed to more intellectually sophisticated ones.

Insects:

Visiting a lake or swamp area from spring to fall one of the most impressive sights is that of dragonflies. This is particularly so when you consider that these beautiful insects are voracious eaters of insects we love to hate, such as mosquitoes. Dragonflies of all sizes and colors can be seen soaring, and any observer paying attention will note that there are often two of them locked into what appears to be, and actually is, a sexual embrace. It has been proven that quite frequently these pairing are homoerotic in nature. Male dragonflies, and the related damselflies, have pinchers that inflict a characteristic damage to the head of females during sex. In 20-80% of males this same damage has been noted that could only have arisen from male-male pairings. The reason why homoerotic behavior occurs in dragonflies and damselflies is not known. However, various explanations have been suggested, including the unavailability of female partners and environmental toxins. Considering how widespread homoerotic behavior is amongst at least male dragonflies and damselflies, it is unlikely that environmental toxins could account for the behavior.

Perhaps the most studied insect on the planet consists of fruit flies, because they are commonly used in genetics research. Homoerotic behavior has been observed and linked to multiple genes influencing courtship and mating behavior. It appears that the genes control behavior via pheromones (chemical messages detected by smell), and by influences on neurological structures. A much more troublesome insect from our perspective, bed bugs, engage in male-male homoerotic behavior. The reason for this is quite clear, being due to how male bed bugs are sexually attracted to and mount others that have just fed. Sexuality in these insects is quite gruesome from a human perspective, with the male piercing a female's abdomen with a needle-like penis. Females have evolved a special structure to reduce injury and accept the sperm, but this adaptation is lacking in males. Consequently, male-male homoerotic behavior can result in death or serious injury to the one mounted.

The more skeptical reader might be thinking that a few insect species of the countless ones on the planet do not show that homoerotic behavior is common in insects. However, such behavior has been observed in numerous insect species, including the common house fly (and other flies such as Tsetse), fleas, wasps, bees, beetles, weevils, butterflies, moths, water bugs such as Water striders, milkweed bugs, locusts, and ants. Think how difficult it would be to establish whether sexual partners are other-sex or same-sex for many insect species. The list of those engaging in homoerotic behavior grows with further careful and unbiased investigations, and it can be confidently stated that such behavior is common amongst these cognitively simple organisms.

Other Invertebrates:

In addition to insects other animals lacking a backbone engage in homoerotic behavior. Certain species of the following types of invertebrates engage in such behavior: Spiders, crabs, octopi, blood flukes, worms, and even yeast. In combination with insects it is difficult to deny that creatures lacking a backbone have a propensity to homoerotic behavior. In almost all cases these organisms are very simple from a cognitive perspective, refuting any suggestion that an animal must be quite intelligent to engage in homoerotic behavior. Octopi are very intelligent being the most cognitively sophisticated of invertebrates, with some demonstrating very advanced problem solving abilities. For example, they have been observed to leave a tank, cross a section of a laboratory to reach a container with a potential meal, unscrew the container lid, remove the meal, and return to their tank. However, other invertebrates are much simpler from a cognitive perspective, proving that intelligence is not a prerequisite for homoerotic behavior.

62

Reptiles & Amphibians:

Amongst reptiles homoerotic behavior is actually quite common, and the reasons for this occurrence are somewhat more obvious than for invertebrates. Male lizards of the genus Teiidae insert their hemipenes into both females and males. Male-male contact of this nature serves to stimulate the normally passive male so that he engages sexually with females. Males take turns with each other to produce the stimulation required for sex with females. Homoerotic stimulation assisting in heterosexual behavior is known as proceptivity enhancement. Female whiptail lizards can actually reproduce asexually creating identical copies of their own self. Female-female sexual contact stimulates ovulation, and when a female is in the low estrogen phase of her cycle she assumes the masculine role engaging with a female in the high estrogen phase. The latter is stimulated to ovulate leading to reproduction if all goes well. When the female, who initially adopted the masculine role, enters the high estrogen phase of her cycle, she takes the female role and is stimulated to ovulate by another female. The wonders of nature never cease to amaze.

In various lizard species there appears to be a territorial/dominance aspect to male-male sexual encounters, with the dominant male mounting a more subordinate one to establish control over a breeding territory. Any females in the area are then for the dominant male. Receptivity reduction is another possible reason for homoerotic behavior in reptiles, whereby the stimulated partner wastes sexual energy leaving more reproductive opportunities for the initiator of this strategy. Regardless of the precise reason, numerous reptile species engage in homoerotic behavior, including various types of iguana, geckos, anole, skinks, snakes, turtles, and of course lizards. Amphibians including frogs and salamanders have also been observed to engage in homoerotic behavior. Although much more cognitively sophisticated than invertebrates (with the exception of octopi) these animals are quite limited cognitively, and certainly compared to mammals and primates. Hence, any remaining notions that homoerotic behavior can only occur in animals with advanced cognitive abilities must be fully dispensed with.

Fish:

Several fish species have been shown to engage in homoerotic behavior. This is particularly interesting because virtually all fish reproduce by spawning, whereby eggs and sperm are released into the water column. Spawning typically involves a male and female making a close approach to each other, swimming upwards and simultaneously releasing their sperm or eggs. Consequently, there is no direct contact involved in fish reproduction for the most part. However, that does not seem to stop some fish from engaging in homoerotic behavior. For example, the male Ten-spined stickleback fish often mimics the female role in copulation with dominant males, perhaps to get them to waste their sperm. When male guppies are confined to an all male group they will court each other even nipping the genital area, an action that characterizes male-female courting. Homoerotic behavior has also been observed in certain species of salmon, sunfish, char, whitefish, topminnow, swordtail, jewel fish, and leaf fish.

Birds:

Homoerotic behavior occurs in many species of birds manifesting in some very dramatic and enduring ways. Back in 1911 George Murray Levick observed Adelie penguins at Cape Adare engaging in same-sex activity.

Influenced by the morals of his time, he described their behavior as "depraved." The report was deemed to be too shocking for public release, and the only copies made were translated into Greek to prevent widespread dissemination of the knowledge. The report came to light a century later and was published in Polar Record in June of 2012. This is fascinating because public awareness of animal homosexuality back then might have led to further research and enlightenment. Moving ahead to modern times, several different species of penguins have been observed to engage in homoerotic pairings. Upwards of 10% of pairing in the wild are between same-sex individuals, and this is for a type of bird that often pairs for life. Same-sex penguin pairings occur in captivity as well. For example, a couple of male Chinstrap penguins named Roy and Silo in the Central Park Zoo in New York City, actually hatched and raised a female chick from a fertile egg they were given to incubate! Male penguin couples have also been noted in zoos in other countries, such as Germany and Japan. The males share nest building and even attempt to incubate stones serving as a substitute for eggs. In Bremerhaven Zoo in Germany, an attempt was made to separate male Humbolt penguin couples and have them mate with females, but the bonds were too strong. In some instance, though, when a female is available one of the males will leave and pair with the female. For example, a pair of male Magellanic penguins who shared a burrow for six years at the San Francisco Zoo and raised a surrogate chick, split when one left for a female that became available when her male partner died.

Male vultures in zoos have also been observed to form homoerotic pairings. At Allwetter Zoo in Muenstar Germany, two male vultures built a nest together. Other vultures picked on them and tried to steal their nest material but they stayed together, at least until staff separated them. At Jerusalem Biblical Zoo two male vultures, named Dashik and Yehuda, practiced what was described as open and energetic sex with each other. They built a nest and took turns incubating an artificial egg. When staff replaced the egg with a baby vulture the couple reared the chick together. Unfortunately for Dashik, Yehuda became interested in a female vulture that was brought into the aviary. Appearing depressed Dashik was moved to a new home where he set up a nest with a female vulture.

Black swans males appear particularly homoerotic, with one-quarter engaging in such behavior. The male pairs work as a team even stealing nests, defending territory, and forming temporary threesomes with females to fertilize and obtain eggs. Once the egg is acquired the female is driven away. Interestingly, the offspring of these male-male pairing are more likely to survive to adulthood than those from other-sex pairing. It appears that male pairs have a greater ability to defend larger territories beneficial for offspring, providing a clear function for homoerotic behavior even of an enduring nature. Supporting the notion that homoerotic pairings can actually increase the survival of chicks, the same occurrence has been noted with male flamingo pairs.

The Andean "cock of the rock" birds show very high levels of male-male sexual activity, even up to 40%. Their name derives from the very colorful brilliant orange plumage on their huge crest. When male birds are adorned in such a flamboyant fashion it is because evolution has produced intense competition for females, and only the showiest get to mate. This occurrence suggests a possible explanation for the high rate of homoerotic behavior observed. An excess of males and intense competition might make heteroerotic pairing an unlikely occurrence for many males. Male-male sexual contact eases social tensions that would otherwise occur between males, due to their highly developed sex drive. Getting some satisfaction, so to speak, the males get along and wait for a chance to reproduce with a female. Aggressive encounters are reduced and social stability increased by the homoerotic male-male encounters. Amongst zebra finches sexually frustrated males will actually adopt female receptive behavior, particularly when rejected by females.

So far the same-sex pairings mentioned have involved male birds, but female pairings are also very common. For example, about 10-15% of female Western gulls pair off with other females. They even demonstrate mounting behavior characteristic of male-female pairs. Now you might wonder how could they reproduce? As it turns out large numbers of eggs are often found in the nests of these female-female pairings, suggesting that both are producing fertile eggs, as evidenced by research on California's Channel Islands. It turns out that the females often have brief sexual encounters with males. Laysan albatrosses of Oahu Hawaii also show high rates of female-female pair bonding, up to 31%. These pairs engage in bill kissing, build nests together, and perform other actions typical of breeding pairs. One pair lasted an amazing 19 years together, truly a long-term marriage! A reason for these pairing might be an excess of females and shortage of males, with the males simply fertilizing the egg during brief encounters. The female same-sex pairings appear to enhance care for offspring, particularly if males are in short supply. In addition, social tensions between females might be too great if they have to compete for males in a system with strictly male-female pairings. The option of female-female pairings reduces social tensions, and also allows for successful rearing of offspring. Similar female-female pairings have also been noted with the larger Royal albatrosses of New Zealand.

Homoerotic behavior and actual pairings have been observed in several other birds including, barn owls, chickens, emu, ravens, seagulls, other gulls than those mentioned, and some songbirds. In Mallard ducks an interesting mechanism known as imprinting plays a role. Baby ducks bond to the first individual they encounter, usually their mother. If you are the first person encountered they will bond to you and follow you around. Young male mallard ducks only exposed to other males during the imprinting period, will grow up to be exclusively homosexual. This unique mechanism producing a homoerotic sexual orientation does not apply to the other bird species reviewed though. In addition, a newly hatched duck with no mother present would not survive in the wild.

Land & Marine Mammals:

Generally speaking the intelligence of mammals is substantially greater than that of birds, and consequently greater flexibility of behavior is seen. Research reveals no shortage of homoerotic behavior, and often of quite a flexible nature. So far we have not witnessed any definitive evidence of exclusive homosexuality, despite how common homoerotic behavior is. There is the example of male Mallard ducks only exposed to males at birth, but in nature this would never result in survival to adulthood. Some isolated couples, such as the male Humbolt penguins mentioned, seem to show a preference for remaining together, but an actual homosexual orientation is uncommon. A mammal species that exclusive homosexuality appears common in is domesticated male sheep (rams), where up to 8% demonstrate a consistent homosexual orientation. These individuals do not mate with females, showing no interest at all throughout their entire life. One potential problem in assuming that this is natural behavior is that these animals are farmed, and as such their behavior has been strongly influenced by humans. For instance, people protect herds that might not otherwise survive in the wild. To say that full homosexual orientation is completely natural we ideally want to see it in animals that are wild.

Arguably the most stereotypically "masculine" of mammals is the African male lion, with its regal mane and tendency to let females do most of the work, while they save their energy for highly robust sex. Shattering the illusion of real "masculinity," male lions mount each other and engage in other sexual behaviors typically reserved for male-female pairings. Male lions appear to engage in these homoerotic relationships to strengthen alliances required to secure mating rights over females. Coalitions of males will routinely defend a territory containing females. Sites that attract prey animals bring female lions, due to the greater likelihood of their offspring surviving at these locations. In order to secure mating rights with females at these prime sites, alliances with other males are necessary.

Elephants are one of the most intelligent animals, actually being able to recognize themselves in a mirror, the so-called mirror test, passed by only a few animal species. Male African and Asian elephants frequently mount each other, and engage in other homoerotic actions such as kissing, trunk intertwining, and placing their trunks in each other's mouth. One individual will extend his trunk along the others back and push forward with his tusks to signify the intent to mount, indicating a clear communication pattern. Of great significance for primate and human homoerotic behavior, as we will see, is how older males will often form a sexual alliance with one or two younger males, an important social dynamic that commonly lasts for years. These individuals support each other when challenges arise. Male-female pairings in contrast tend to be very brief. Female-female pairings are also common, and homoerotic interactions occur frequently in both sexes. Sexual contact between Asian elephants in captivity involves same-sex individuals 45% of the time.

Male giraffes demonstrate very high rates of homoerotic behavior, actually more than heteroerotic! One study revealed that an incredible 94% of mountings involved two males. They commonly tongue kiss, nuzzle each other's neck, hug, and actively court. Unions tend to be short-term and it has been noted that they predominately involve young males. It appears that these males are practicing their mating technique to get it right before trying it out on a female. The small size of giraffe herds might play a role in that the number of available female partners is often limited, and a male does not want to mess things up with awkward sexual behavior, thereby losing the opportunity to mate with a female. Supporting this notion, only 1% of observed same-sex mounts involve females.

Spotted hyenas are very aggressive animals, and it appears that the level of testosterone males and females are exposed to in the womb, greatly influences their degree of aggressiveness—Higher levels of testosterone produce higher levels of aggression. Same-sex mounting establishes dominance-subordinate rankings with the mounting individual being more dominant. Dominant individuals have preferential access to partners for reproduction. Both male and female same-sex mounting occurs, but more often between females. Female-female mounting also frequently occurs in other species such as cows, referred to as "bulling" by dairy farmers. Mounting behavior appears to be a sign that the cow is in heat. Same-sex mountings are actually very common amongst land mammals seemingly serving different functions, such as the establishment of dominant-subordinate status as with spotted hyenas, practice for adult sex in male juvenile giraffe, and an expression of receptivity as with cows. Additional land mammals demonstrating homoerotic behavior include dogs, domestic cats, polecats, goats, pigs, horses, antelopes, red deer, bisons, bears, caribou, foxes, rabbits, koala, raccoons, porcupines, marmosets, rats, and mice.

Considering the number and diversity of land mammals that engage in homoerotic behavior, it will not come as a surprise to learn that marine mammals also do so, and sometimes in very unique ways. Amongst bottlenose dolphins same-sex pairings are very common. Interestingly, at times these relationships suggest more of an orientation to homoerotic behavior, such as one 17-year romance, and an all-male pod of dolphins. Some dolphins appear more bisexual with relationships flexibly shifting from same-sex to other-sex. Females have been observed engaging in beak-genital propulsion, where one individual inserts her beak in the genital opening of another while gently swimming forward. Males will rub their genitals against those of another male, an action that sometimes leads to them swimming belly to belly inserting the penis in the other's genital slit or anus. A key function served by these homoerotic relationships appears to be bond formation that can last for a lifetime. Same-sex individuals who form such bonds often help protect each other, and males appear to assist those they have sexually bonded with in locating females to reproduce with. The latter occurrence strongly highlights how homoerotic relationships can actually advance reproduction. These relationships, between males at least, might also reduce aggression serving a tension reduction function. Interestingly, this function appears to play a role in cross-species homoerotic encounters—When a pod of bottlenose dolphins encounter the closely related Atlantic spotted dolphins, males from both pods will sometimes engage in homoerotic behavior rather than aggression!

Amazon River dolphins or boto are the only animal known to perform "nasal sex," with both same-sex and other-sex individuals. This form of sexual contact involves penetration of the blowhole, equivalent to the nostril of other mammals, providing a very unique form of sexual stimulation. Same-sex contact also involves the use of snout, flippers, and genital rubbing. Male boto have also been observed to have sexual relationships with males from the tucuxi species, a small porpoise. This is similar to the sexual interactions between bottlenose dolphins and Atlantic spotted dolphins. Other dolphin species and also orcas have been observed engaging in homoerotic encounters. The evidence is then indisputable that a very wide range of land and marine mammals engage in homoerotic behavior, with some hint of a preference in a few species.

Primates:

Both lesser apes consisting of most primate species, and the greater apes closely related to humans (chimpanzees, bonobos, gorillas, and orangutans), engage in homoerotic behavior. In many instances this behavior is of the mounting variety, but it also takes some very complex forms. Baboon and rhesus monkeys share a similar form of social organization to our hunting/gathering ancestors, living in small groups moving about in search of food. Baboon and rhesus troops are organized hierarchically based on dominant-subordinate relationships, the power structure becoming evident when a threat such as a predator appears. The dominant males remain in the center with the females and young individuals, while subordinate males guard the periphery. Understandably, the chance of injury and death is greater for these peripheral males. Homoerotic alliances commonly form between peripheral males, and in some instances more dominant males. Mutual embracing, grooming, penis display and touching, mutual masturbation, oral stimulation, and mounting, all have been observed. Homoerotic alliances involving subordinate peripheral males assist in survival when attacks occur, and might also raise their testosterone levels enhancing the likelihood of successful heteroerotic mating. When a homoerotic alliance occurs between dominant and subordinate males, the latter gains not only an ally in the event of an attack, but an elevation in social status affording a greater chance of mating with a female.

Rhesus males also engage in homoerotic behavior with young individuals who attempt to enter into a new group. If the young male bonds sexually with a dominant male, then acceptance into the new troop is much more likely allowing access to resources. Homoerotic relationships that appear to be very strong and enduring also occur between female rhesus monkeys. Both partners gain an ally in the event of confrontations, and when one is more dominant the subordinate one rises in social standing. A similar pattern occurs with female Japanese macaques. Several species of baboons, macaques, gibbons, and langurs, amongst other lesser primates, also commonly engage in homoerotic behavior.

Of the great apes the most sexual and homoerotic are the bonobos, often referred to as pygmy chimps, given that they are closely related to chimpanzees but slightly smaller. By all accounts 100% of bonobos engage in homoerotic, and also heteroerotic behavior. Colorful

73

descriptions have been applied such as they make love and not war, and use the language of love rather than the language of aggression. Indeed, it appears that a very prominent reason for homoerotic behavior, and sexual actions more generally, is to reduce tensions and reconcile conflicts, thereby enhancing social stability. Most aggressive encounters involve male-male and female-female interactions, and homoerotic behavior can rapidly diffuse, and even prevent these encounters. For example, when a novel object is presented to most primates, conflicts often arise based on the potential value of the new object. Interest is peeked and investigation of the potential source of reward occurs. With bonobos the appearance of a novel object, such as a cardboard box, initiates sexual contact such as brief mounting before the object is explored. This sexual contact diffuses tension and prevents aggression. Following a minor aggressive encounter sexual contact is frequent, fostering reconciliation and preventing an escalation of aggression to more intense levels.

Bonobos also form alliances with each other based on homoerotic encounters, and these alliances are crucial to their success. Indeed, an individual who does not form alliances based on homoerotic relationships cannot function in the social group. Such an individual would lose out when it comes to securing important resources including reproductive opportunities. There is some suggestion that more exclusive homosexuality occurs with bonobos, but it appears that they are all capable of both homoerotic and heteroerotic encounters. Homoerotic behavior is also present in other great ape species. For example, male-male mounting takes place with chimpanzees and mountain gorillas. Nor is the mounting stereotypical front-to-back, with front-to-front being noted in mountain gorillas at least. Adult male chimpanzees frequently groom each other, with fondling of the more dominant male's scrotum. Grooming of the genital-anal region stimulates erections in male chimpanzees of all ages. Male-male grooming strengthens social bonds, and the alliances formed appear to increase actual reproductive success. Homoerotic actions easing social tensions, repairing damaged relationships, and establishing alliances, definitely occur amongst the great apes. Homoerotic behavior in primates evidently serves several functions as with other animal species.

WHAT WE CAN LEARN FROM ANIMAL HOMOSEXUALITY:

The commonality and diversity of homoerotic behavior demonstrated in countless animals species ranging from insects to primates, clearly indicates that such behavior is the norm and not the exception. Species covering the full spectrum of cognitive abilities engage in homoerotic behavior, proving that such behavior is not dependent upon intelligence. With greater cognitive sophistication comes more complex forms of homoerotic behavior, but it does not alter the frequency of such behavior. The more that researchers look with an unbiased attitude, the more evidence for animal "homosexuality" that is found. This in itself strongly implies that homoerotic behavior does not detract from reproduction and evolutionary fitness. Supporting this notion is how rare exclusive homosexual relationships are in the animal world, compared to homoerotic behavior. The evidence indicates that homoerotic actions do not detract from reproduction, and in some instances definitely enhance evolutionary fitness.

Homoerotic behavior serves several functions, some related to reproduction and others not, at least directly. Specific benefits that we have seen include stimulation for ovulation and heteroerotic encounters, receptivity reduction in a competitor, establishment of dominant status, greater success in defending a nest or territory necessary for successful rearing of offspring, expression of sexual receptivity in females, practice for heteroerotic encounters, tension reduction and reconciliation both promoting greater social stability, and alliance formation. Even one or two of these benefits provides a solid evolutionary rationale for homoerotic behavior, but combined the advantageous to many animals species cannot be ignored, as they apparently have been by many theorists and researchers attempting to explain the evolutionary paradox of homosexuality. If there are so many benefits to homoerotic behavior, it might well be the case that there is no paradox. However, before we can conclude that this is the case we have to examine human sexual behavior, and try to understand why some individuals display a homosexual orientation.

DIMENSIONS OF SEXUAL ORIENTATION

A key to characterizing the nature of something is determining whether it is organized discretely or continuously. Discrete refers to an either/or aspect whereby something is one or the other. For example, do you have brown or blue eyes? Dimensional involves a continuum ranging from little to a lot of the given characteristic. For instance, how aggressive are you? Some people are slightly aggressive getting angry and acting on it only with severe provocation, others more moderate in this motivation, while there are those who attack in response to the slightest of challenges or when an opportunity to acquire something valuable arises. It turns out that most things in nature, and certainly psychology, tend to be dimensional. Even the example of eye color while seemingly fully discrete, appears less so upon closer examination. Most people can be separated into those having brown and blue eyes, but what about those with green or hazel color? Eye color is based on a combination of one gene from the mother and one from the father. Brown (B) is dominant meaning that it expresses itself whenever present, whereas blue (b) is recessive only fully showing in the absence of a brown gene. Hence, to have blue eyes a person inherits a blue gene from both parents (bb). The other three possible combinations consist of a brown gene from each parent (BB), a brown gene from the mother and blue from the father (Bb), and a brown gene from the father and blue gene from the mother (also Bb). The BB gene combination results in a brown-eyed individual, as does the Bb combination given that B expresses itself whenever present. However, some people with Bb end up having green or hazel eyes related to a blending of brown and blue genes. So even for a simple one-gene trait involving dominant and recessive genes, there is some degree of dimensionality.

Charles Darwin discovered the principle of natural selection. Essentially, variation in genetically encoded traits results in different outcomes, depending on environmental influences. Versions of traits that are most suited or beneficial for a given environment, are preferentially passed on because they help those with the trait survive and reproduce, thereby increasing the frequency of that version in succeeding generations. Less adaptive versions result in diminished reproductive success, translating into reduced frequency in succeeding generations. For example, around 4 million years ago our ancestors began walking upright, an adaptation to shrinking forests that were replaced by open grassy savannah with limited trees. The version of the mobility trait that made some individuals better at walking upright was most adaptive for the changed environment, fostering greater success at surviving and reproducing. Consequently, it was passed on to succeeding generations more frequently than versions only allowing the individual to walk on all fours. Trait variation is the substance acted upon by natural selection allowing for evolution. Continuums provide for trait variation, whereas discrete entities do not. What this means is that if nature was organized discretely, and not continuously, there would be no variation, and hence no evolution. Traits lacking any variation (truly discrete) either persist if selection pressures favor the given characteristics or perish if not favored, an either or scenario. Ample trait variation provided by a continuous organization of forms, allow for the most adaptive variant/s to become more represented in succeeding generations, the hallmark of natural selection and evolution.

Not surprisingly then, almost all physical and behavioral characteristics are organized continuously. Most physical characteristics result from the expression of multiple genes encoding for proteins making up the structure. Demonstrating a self-enhancing species-centric perspective, scientists once assumed that we have many more protein encoding genes than lesser organisms. Shattering this grand illusion, the Human Genome Project has revealed a total of 20,000-25,000 protein encoding genes, approximately the same number as the simple roundworm, C. elegans! As it turns out, it is not just the presence or absence of protein encoding genes that counts, but regulation of these genes by others that turn them on and off at the appropriate time. These regulatory genes can be influenced by internal and environmental signals, a process known as epigenetics. Throughout time there has been debate regarding whether traits are due to nature (genes) or nurture (environmental influences). For many characteristics beyond those involving single genes, there appears to be a combination of genetic and environmental factors, with the environment influencing the activity of regulatory genes (epigenetics). For example, the intrusion of a virus into the body activates regulatory genes, in turn stimulating the expression of protein encoding genes involved in immune system responses, such as antibody formation.

With multiple genes for most characteristics, both genetic and environmental inputs, and epigenetic regulation, it would be virtually impossible for most physical characteristics to be discrete. When it comes to behaviors that typically involve numerous environmental inputs, a range of expressions is almost guaranteed.

Although dimensionality is perfectly sensible, there has been a distinct tendency for people and researchers to see human characteristics as being discrete. For example, investigations into countless diseases have seen geneticists searching for the single illusive gene that produces it. One example is for schizophrenia, where we frequently hear media reports of a schizophrenia gene being discovered that will lead to effective interventions. Typically, the discovery does not stand up to further scrutiny, and even when it does the influence is highly limited. Perhaps this is why schizophrenia has been described as the graveyard of geneticists. However, the same problem applies to genetic investigations into many conditions, and it is only recently that we are seeing a real appreciation of how multiple genes are usually involved. Furthermore, the role of epigenetic factors is only starting to be unraveled.

With many behavioral occurrences people tend to see, or wish to see, a discrete aspect. For example, "He is effeminate and gay," or, "She is masculine but straight." Life seems simpler and easier to process if we can dispense with the complications. Unfortunately, this simplified processing leaves us in the dark about what is actually occurring, and frequently leads to distorted views. For example, "If he's gay, how can he be masculine? According to the discrete perspective people are masculine, feminine, gay, or straight. Nice and simple, but as we are about to see, there is much more to the story than a discrete perspective suggests.

Before looking at dimensions of sexual orientation, it is worth considering whether or not there is any aspect of sexuality that is discrete. One potential candidate is gender identity. Do you consider yourself male or female, or somewhere in between? The last part of this question seems absurd because most of us perceive ourselves as clearly male or female, gender identity typically aligning with male and female biology. The vast majority of homosexual men identify as being male, and homosexual women as female. Many transgender individuals tend to see themselves as being male or female, in this instance the gender identity other than their biological sex. To bring biological sex into alignment with gender identity many transgender people engage in hormonal and surgical interventions, or at least fantasize about changing when the means are not present. Intersex conditions covered in the transgender chapter detract somewhat from purely discrete biological sex. In addition, gender identity is not all about biological sex, with masculine and feminine characteristics playing a major role.

Masculinity/femininity turns out to be highly dimensional in nature, with people having varying degrees of each quality. Imagine if you had to be completely masculine or feminine, super macho or sweet as candy. Outside of some Hollywood stereotype no one matches this description. So there is a range of masculine and feminine behavior, involving a continuum from highly masculine to highly feminine. Most people rate somewhere between these extremes. But is this way of organizing masculinity and femininity accurate? Let us consider the implications. If masculinity and femininity are arranged on opposite ends of a continuum, higher levels of one must trade off for lower levels of the other. Hence, if a person is very masculine, then that individual cannot be at all feminine. Conversely, if someone is very feminine, then he or she cannot be masculine. In addition, people who rank in the middle of the scale cannot be that masculine or feminine—Not as feminine as those at the feminine pole, and not as masculine as those at the masculine pole. Hence, as reasonable as this form of dimensional organization might initially sound, it does not capture the reality of masculinity and femininity. Higher levels of masculinity and femininity do not trade off against each other, with some people having both very masculine and feminine traits, such as being aggressive and also highly nurturing. Furthermore, moderate levels of one do not necessarily predict similar levels of the other.

A consideration of the characteristic of masculine and feminine behavior will help bring this issue into better focus. The terms masculine and feminine include several different categories of characteristics, summarized by Michael Shively and John De Cocco in their article, Components of sexual identity:

Physical attributes—Consists of secondary sexual characteristics such as presence or absence of body hair.

Physical condition—Healthy men and women are seen as being more masculine and feminine, respectively. Average weight women are viewed as more feminine, than very overweight or too thin women.

Mannerisms—Refers to how an individual moves, sits, or stands. More uncontrolled hand movements increase the perception of femininity.

Adornment—What a person selects to put on including tattoos, jewelry, and clothing.

Personality traits—Masculinity is often associated with aggression, assertiveness, and confidence, whereas femininity is typically linked to nurturance and softness.

Grooming—Men and women are seen as being more masculine and feminine, respectively, when they are well kept in terms of clothing and hair.

Speech and vocabulary—Consists of voice inflection including pitch and tone, and also the words used in speech with slang seen as more masculine.

Social interaction—How a person relates to others in social situations, with more dominant and in control behavior typically being viewed as masculine.

Interests—Some activities are seen as more traditionally masculine, such as team sports and others such as opera more feminine.

Habits—These diverse and specific behaviors include nail biting, seen as more feminine, and cigar smoking considered to be more masculine.

With such an extensive range of feminine and masculine characteristics, it is almost inconceivable that a person could rate fully masculine or feminine in all. What about the overweight male who has a deep voice and bites his nails watching sports? Likewise, what about the loud and assertive woman who wears feminine clothing and jewelry? If a person is aggressive does that mean that he or she cannot show any nurturing behavior? Placing people on a single continuum ranging from highly feminine to highly masculine simply does not capture the complexity of femininity and masculinity. We would be forced to conceptualize masculinity and femininity like a Hollywood stereotype to make it work at all, and as we all know real life can be much more complex than movie portrayals. So far then we have determined that masculinity and femininity are continuous as opposed to discrete, and that a single dimensional representation does not work, but how are we to capture this important aspect of gender identity?

Might two separate dimensions of masculinity and femininity work, with each person ranking somewhere along both dimensions? If so, then it is possible for an individual to be both highly masculine and feminine, even at the same time. For example, a person acts aggressively towards someone attempting to harm a child, but also consoles the youngster. Both aggressive and nurturing behavior is displayed at the same time. Perhaps a man has effeminate mannerisms while dressing very masculine. Masculinity and femininity then do not have to trade off against each other, instead coexisting. The various masculine characteristics can be combined to produce a ranking on the masculinity dimension, and the feminine characteristics to yield a placement on the femininity dimension. Scales ranging from, Not at all to Very, can be set for both masculinity and femininity, as with the Bem Sex Role Inventory. Those who are equally masculine and feminine might be viewed as androgynous overall.

A major implication of two separate dimensions for masculinity and femininity is that people no longer have to worry about being masculine or feminine, as everyone is both! We all show a blend of masculine and feminine traits. Some people rank high on both, with such individuals showing intensely masculine and feminine behavior. On the opposite end of the two dimensional organization, some individuals rank low on these traits, as with a person who does not dress or act either feminine or masculine. Understanding masculinity and femininity as two separate dimensions adds complexity, thereby challenging our motivation to keep perceptions simple. However, it greatly diminishes the stress of feeling that we have to be either masculine or feminine. It also helps reduce persecution based on perceived differences. For example, does it make any sense to criticize or bully someone for being feminine, when you also show feminine characteristics as well? Considering that gender identity is influenced by masculine and feminine characteristics, it cannot be fully discrete either, and indeed there are many individuals who identify with both genders to varying degrees. As covered in the transgender chapter, some "transgender" people have a dual (or neither) gender identity, adding complexities to gender identity that we would prefer not to have. After all, the perspective of gender identity strictly aligning with discrete biological sex, or being reversed, is easier to understand.

Sexual orientation is another major component of sexuality that appears continuous, despite the desire of many to simplify it as gay or straight. From a discrete perspective, though, it is difficult to envision how bisexuals fit in. Perhaps we should assume that there is no such thing as bisexuality, such individuals really being gay but not yet accepting it. This is the very reaction that many bisexuals I have seen in my practice experience. They are often not understood by anyone other than fellow bisexuals. A typical sentiment is that while there is the plus of more potential partners, given their dual sexual interest, rejection and skepticism by others is a major stress. The perceived rejection impacts adversely on their self-esteem, making some feel lesser than either gays or straights, or worse, deceivers by believing that they are interested in both sexes. Many join bi-groups to feel accepted and understood. So the simplified perception of gay and straight, while easing brain work has some very undesirable consequences on those not fitting into this neat arrangement. It might be suggested that we include a third discrete bisexual category, but since this incorporates homosexual and heterosexual orientations, it does not work as a fully discrete scenario.

Responding to the notion that human sexual orientation might be discrete and not continuous, Kinsey and colleagues state in Sexual behavior In The Human Male (1948), "Males do not represent two discrete populations, heterosexual and homosexual. The world is not divided into sheep and goats. It is a fundamental of taxonomy that nature rarely deals with discrete categories...The living world is a continuum in each and every one of its aspects." They add in Sexual Behavior In The Human Female (1953), "It is a characteristic of the human mind that tries to dichotomize in its classification of phenomena...Sexual behavior is either normal or abnormal, socially acceptable or unacceptable, heterosexual or homosexual; and many persons do not want to believe that there are gradations in these matters from one to the other extreme." These statements capture how nature and certainly human sexuality is organized in a continuous fashion, while our perception of discrete categories is an illusion arising from a psychological inclination to dichotomize when classifying. Discrete entities are easier to process mentally, accuracy being traded off for simplicity. A formal statement that might be referred to as the "continuum principle" is warranted, considering our automatic tendency to apply discreteness to what are almost universally continuous variables— Natural phenomena tend to occur on a continuum and any instance of hypothesized discreteness requires unassailable proof. Hence, any researcher or theorist positing discrete forms of sexual orientation must provide unambiguous evidence. No researcher to date has been able to do so.

Assuming that sexual orientation, like masculinity/femininity, is dimensional how is it organized—One dimension or two? Alfred Kinsey and his colleagues, Pomeroy and Martin, devised a single dimension scale for sexual orientation and administered it to many people. The Kinsey Scale, as it is known, ranges from 0 to 6:

0-Exclusive heterosexuality

1-Predominantly heterosexual, only incidentally homosexual

2-Predominantly heterosexual, but more than incidentally homosexual

3-Equally heterosexual and homosexual

4-Predominantly homosexual, but more than incidentally heterosexual

5-Predominantly homosexual, only incidentally heterosexual

6-Exclusively homosexual

X Non-sexual

The initial results were presented in Sexual Behavior In The Human Male. According to the Kinsey Reports, 11.6% of white males between the ages of 20-35 rated 3 indicating a bisexual orientation. 10% of males were "more or less exclusively homosexual for at least three years between the ages of 16 and 55." Regarding women aged 20-35, 7% rated 3, and a similar number emerged as more or less exclusively homosexual, as reported in Sexual Behavior In The Human Female.

A major problem with a single dimension for sexual orientation is how to manage asexuality. Asexuality has been described as the fourth sexual orientation after heterosexual, homosexual, and bisexual. "A" refers to the absence of something so asexual means the absence of sexuality. Some individuals have an extremely low motivation for sex rarely thinking about it and showing no real interest, as difficult as that might seem to many of us. So what happens when you try and fit an asexual orientation into the Kinsey Scale? If you are to place asexuality on the actual scale the only option is at 3, the same value as for full bisexuality. Of course this is ludicrous because bisexuals are sexually motivated and for both sexes, a far cry from no or little motivation for either. Hence, Kinsey was forced to create an X rating off the scale (non-sexual).

There are further problems with Kinsey's scale and its depiction of human sexuality, a major one being that homosexuality and heterosexuality trade off against each other. If you rate a 6 it means that you are strictly homosexual and cannot engage in any heterosexual behavior or fantasy. In some instances people who function as a homosexual or heterosexual, engage in a relationship that is not in keeping with their primary preference. Sexuality can be quite fluid shifting over time, despite what many people think. Of course it could be argued that a person then shifts on the rating scale. More difficult to reconcile with the Kinsey Scale, and other single dimension sexual orientation scales, is the implication that a high homosexual motivation precludes a high heterosexual motivation, and vice versa. How then are we to explain those with high motivation for both males and females? If you respond by saying they are bisexual and rate a 3 it does work, because on a single dimension bisexuals must be less homosexual than exclusive homosexuals, and less heterosexual than exclusive heterosexuals! This is a clearly false scenario as many bisexual individuals are strongly motivated both homosexually and heterosexually, and at least as much so as those with more exclusive orientations. So even though a single dimension of sexual orientation represents a huge leap in our understanding over discrete categories, it still fails to capture the nature of this crucial aspect of sexuality.

In the case of masculinity and femininity we learned how two dimensions, one for masculinity and one for femininity work well. Might the same apply to sexual orientation? Each person then ranks on separate scales for homo and hetero motivation, both ranging from low to high. At this point it is important to shift the terms homosexual and heterosexual to homoerotic and heteroerotic, respectively. This name change is warranted for at least two reasons. First, the terms homosexual and heterosexual are loaded with numerous connotations that can prevent or limit perspective shifts, even if those changes more accurately capture the nature of human sexuality. For example many people consider homosexual and heterosexual to be fixed states, a perspective that limits any possibility of flexibility in sexual orientation. Second, there are actually two aspects of our focus when it comes to members of the same or other sex—Social and sexual. Applying naming that captures these important aspects then helps us understand attractions to both sexes. Hence, there are homosocial, heterosocial, homoerotic, and heteroerotic dimensions. An example will demonstrate how these dimensions play out. A man might be strongly sexually drawn to women, but cannot stand socializing with them preferring the company of men. This person is then characterized by a high heteroerotic motivation, low heterosocial motivation, and high homosocial motivation. The description does not let us comment on his homoerotic motivation. If we learn that he has some desire in this regard, then we can add that his homoerotic motivation is in the low to moderate range. For the two erotic and two social dimensions, a person can be rated on scales each ranging from low to high. We will focus on the erotic dimensions.

Getting back to the question of whether or not two separate dimensions for sexual orientation work better than a single one, we must consider the potential advantages to distinct homoerotic and heteroerotic dimensions, and scales to assess them. One clear advantage is that the problem of asexuality is easily solved, because such a person simply rates at the lowest end of both scales, reflecting no or next to no erotic interest in either sex. A further advantage is that bisexuals will separate from asexuals, ranking above the lowest range on both scales and having significant homoerotic and heteroerotic motivation. This represents a massive leap forward from conceptualizing both asexuals and bisexuals at the mid-point of a single dimension, or representing asexuality off the scale as an X. The two dimensional framework also eliminates the clearly false scenario of bisexuals being less motivated than those with a preference for one sex over the other. A bisexual individual can rate at the highest point for both homoerotic and heteroerotic motivations, expressed as robust attraction for both sexes.

Scales that capture the two-dimensional nature of human sexuality have been developed, such as one by Michael Storms plotting homoerotic and heteroerotic motivations on a chart with horizontal and vertical axes. "Hetero-eroticism" is rated on the horizontal axis from low to high, and "homo-eroticism" is placed on the vertical axis, also from low to high. According to this representation asexuals are low on both motivations, bisexuals are high on both, and heterosexuals and homosexuals high on the motivation consistent with their preference, and low on the one that is inconsistent with their preference. Despite its sophistication, this precise organization is problematic in that it does not readily allow for low ratings other than for asexuals. What about bisexuals with fairly low motivation for both sexes, homosexuals with higher but limited motivation for same-sex individuals, and heterosexuals with higher but restricted motivation for other-sex partners? Separate side-by-side homoerotic and heteroerotic dimensions appear to make more sense, with asexuals at the very low end of both, homosexuals having higher same-sex motivation regardless of the precise levels, heterosexuals higher other-sex motivation regardless of the precise levels, and bisexuals with variable but substantial motivation for both sexes.

The Sexual Orientation Grid by Fritz Klein goes beyond ratings for homoerotic and heterorotic dimensions, adding other components, such as how sexual motivation can shift over time, and also rating homosocial and heterosocial motivations. The grid incorporates different dimensions at three points in a person's life—Past, present, and idealized future. The dimensions consist of sexual attraction, sexual behavior, sexual fantasies, emotional preference, social preference, lifestyle preference, and self-identification, with ratings from 1-7 (other-sex only/heterosexual only to same-sex only/homosexual only). While Klein's grid does provide a rich description of behavior and preferences linked to sexual orientation, there are several limitations. One problem being that by trying to provide more dimensions the model ironically might not include enough dimensions, such as age, and masculine/feminine behavior.

Of even greater significance, the dimensions proposed appear to be measuring the same construct. Factor analysis is a statistical technique identifying clusters based on relationships between the components of a cluster. For example, pipes, fittings, and faucets will cluster based on the common plumbing relationship, whereas fork, spoon, and knife will cluster together as eating utensils. A factor analytic study by Weinrich and colleagues using 2 samples, found that one factor (cluster) loaded on all of the grid's 21 components (3 for past, present, and idealized future and the 7 dimensions), meaning that they are all measuring the same construct or dimension. A second factor emerged consisting of social and emotional preferences, indicating that these "dimensions" are measuring something other than sexual orientation. A likely reason for these results is that Klein's "dimensions" probably only constitute descriptors of sexual orientation dimensions (and dimensions for social and emotional preferences). For example, sexual attraction, sexual behavior, sexual fantasies, lifestyle preference, and self-identification, might only describe sexual orientation dimensions and not constitute distinct entities. Supporting this assertion is the finding by Priebe and Svedin that different measures of sexual orientation (identity, attraction, and behavior) are highly linked with each other.

Approximately 200 or so scales have been devised to rate sexual orientation, many incorporating separate homoerotic and heteroerotic motivations. One reason for the number and diversity of scales pertains to how homoerotic and heteroerotic motivations are assessed. Some like Kinsey and Storms believe that erotic fantasy content or "scripts" is the key criteria, whereas others believe that actual behaviors and engagement are more important. Perhaps the most optimal way is to evaluate both behavior and fantasy, giving preferential weight to the latter for reasons made clear in the Erotic Fantasy chapter. Five or seven point scales ranging from extremely low to extremely high can be applied to evaluate homoerotic and heteroerotic motivations, considering both behavior and fantasy. Stronger weightings should be applied to erotic fantasy, likely in the 2-3 times range, although research will have to establish the optimal weighting. Summed scores on the behavior and weighted erotic fantasy scales provide a measure of homoerotic and heteroerotic motivations.

Regardless of the precise criteria applied to assess a person's homoerotic and heteroerotic motivation, an entirely new understanding of sexual orientation emerges, given that people no longer need to think in either/or terms. Everyone has two biologically based dimensions of sexual orientation—Heteroerotic and homoerotic. This implies that we all have a capacity, or possibly even a propensity, to engage in homoerotic acts. Understanding sexual orientation in this way should in itself diminish criticisms and persecution of homosexuals—Criticizing or persecuting someone for having what you also possess is less likely to occur, than for something you do not have and also resent. For example, criticizing someone for having a beard is ludicrous if you also have one, but is more understandable if you lack a beard and hate the look of them. With everyone having the capacity, and likely some non-zero degree of motivation for homoerotic behavior, persecution of homosexuals is ludicrous. Knowledge often leads to further questions and a mystery that arises with our improved understanding of sexual orientation, is why would we have two dimensions, and in particular a homoerotic one? If sex is all about reproduction, then we should just have one heterosexual dimension. Nice and simple like our brains prefer. The fact, and it is a fact given that discrete and single dimensional representations do not work, that we have both homoerotic and heteroerotic dimensions, suggests that there must be a purpose to same-sex behavior. Our goal now is to explore the purposes of homoerotic behavior. Heteroerotic requires much less explaining given that it is a requirement for reproduction.

PURPOSES OF HOMOEROTIC BEHAVIOR

If a dimension of functioning exists in nature it is a fairly safe bet that there is some evolutionary value to it. Nature rarely wastes energy and resources laying down a continuum of behavioral capacity, when the behavior does not serve a purpose. A good example of this principle resides in dimensions of temperament/personality. Temperament is a rudimentary form of personality that we are born with. Based on extensive research by many investigators over several decades, Costa and McCrea presented a 5-factor model of temperament/personality that has come to be known as the "Big 5." These five dimensions consist of:

Introversion/extroversion—Refers to how inwardly versus outwardly directed a person's behavior is, with introverts being very self-focused and extroverts highly outgoing and sociable.

Reactivity—Pertains to how strongly an individual reacts to external and internal stimuli, particularly when the occurrence is unexpected. This is often described as emotional stability, but from an evolutionary perspective reactivity makes more intuitive sense, with emotional stability following from it (highly reactive lower emotional stability).

Openness to experience—As it sounds, this dimension refers to how well a person embraces novel experiences and opportunities, with a range from intense avoidance all the way to eagerly approaching.

94

Conscientiousness—Higher levels provide the capacity for task completion while lower levels limit involvement.

Agreeableness—Indicates how accommodating and compromising a person tends to be.

Each of these five dimensions of temperament/-personality express themselves at a very young age. For example, even infant and toddlers differ in how strongly they react to unexpected stimuli, the extent that they prefer to play alone versus interact with others, and how easy or difficult they are to engage and interact with. Openness to experience and conscientiousness are also evident from a very early age, with young children highly open to experiences moving towards novel objects and events, and those closed to experience adhering to the familiar. Conscientious children tend to finish tasks they have started, while those low on this dimension start something and quickly move on without completing anything. With age a person's relative standing on each of these dimensions becomes more fixed, the overall combination characterizing their personality.

The question arises as to why nature would invest the energy and effort to ensure that we all develop these dimensions of personality? The general answer is that each of them served a useful function during our evolution influencing evolutionary fitness, or the chances of surviving and reproducing. Introversion-extroversion is an important guide to social behavior, and our evolution in hunting-gathering groups ensured the importance of socializing. Reactions to danger or threats in the physical and social environments had a major impact on survival. Novel experiences offered the potential for reward, but also risk, and how a person navigated these opportunities would certainly have influenced the probability of surviving and reproducing. With our intelligence we developed strategies for survival, such as weapon preparation and hunting techniques, and the completion of these tasks would often have influenced success and survival. Living within social settings we had to adjust to other people and be somewhat agreeable, but if too much so a person could be taken advantage of. Hence, how agreeable or disagreeable we are influenced outcomes in the social environment.

So then you might say why not just have the optimal level of the given dimension in everyone and spare the dimension part? The answer is that environmental circumstances dictate the optimal level on each dimension, and these circumstances can and do fluctuate. For example, in a group of fairly placid mostly introverted individuals having an extroverted more socially dominant nature can be rewarding, but in a group of hostile extroverts a more introverted stance can prevent ostracism. A highly reactive nature can save a person from a crocodile attack at a watering hole, but in a safe environment it leads to many false alarms and wasted energy, that could have been better allocated to acquiring resources. If an environment offers important resources without much danger involved in securing them, a high degree of openness to experience is most adaptive, but in a dangerous environment offering few rewards being closed to experience is more adaptive. If the environment has many complex challenges, and task completion is essential to survival, then a high degree of conscientiousness is best. However, if the environment is less challenging, and/or the task completion does not really influence outcomes, wasting energy on completing them is not adaptive. In a cooperative social setting being agreeable is often optimal, but in a social environment where there are a lot of cheaters being disagreeable can safeguard resources.

Hence, the adaptive value of a given level on each of the five dimensions varies with circumstances. Since evolution could never predict the exact circumstances, each of us has been endowed with a point or narrow range on these dimensions. Those fortunate enough to have the optimal level of each for their particular environment tend to do better than those with less optimal levels, although since circumstances vary throughout life, the optimal level at a given point in time in one setting might not be so at a later time in another setting. Furthermore, many people have at least a small range of capacity on each dimension, and can override their natural proclivities by using intelligence and conscious reasoning. For example, a highly introverted person can overcome their proclivity to refrain from being socially outgoing, and become an accomplished public speaker or performer. An individual might also decide to ignore their harm avoidance voice and take on a novel experience. Via these temperament/personality dimensions and intelligence, nature has greatly advanced our capacity to cope with the social and physical environments. Might dimensions of sexuality work in a similar fashion?

Masculinity and femininity dimensions provide for a range of different behaviors as we have seen. Of particular relevance to our evolution are aggression and nurturing behavior, typically viewed as masculine and feminine, respectively. The capacity to engage in both of these behaviors is adaptive for all of us. For example, if you or your child is attacked an aggressive defense can prevent severe injury or death. Likewise, nurturing a child in need can prevent emotional and physical damage. The masculinity dimension provides the capacity for aggression, while the femininity dimension allows for nurturing behavior, at least as traditionally conceived.

Although both forms of behavior are valuable, the precise degree that is adaptive varies with social and physical environmental circumstances. For instance, if you are in a hostile physical environment with numerous predatory animals and competing hunting/gathering groups, a higher level of aggression might be required for survival. In a low threat environment a higher level of aggression serves no purpose, simply wasting energy and encouraging retaliatory attacks. If you have children to look after a high level of nurturing ability is more adaptive, than if you do not have children. Consequently, much as with dimensions of temperament/personality, the precise degree of masculinity and femininity each individual is endowed with varies, the adaptive value of the given level being determined by environmental circumstances.

So far this whole process appears sound, but what about for the dimensions of heteroerotic and homoerotic behavior? Having some heteroerotic motivation clearly makes sense, because reproduction will be less likely if there is none. However, why would people vary in heteroerotic motivation given that a higher level should enhance reproductive success? Having a high level of heteroerotic motivation appears to be a better thing from a perspective of passing on our genes and hence evolutionary fitness. Then there is the problem of homoerotic motivation that at first, or even second, glance does not really make sense. Why would we be motivated for homoerotic behavior when reproduction does not occur, and in fact it might take effort and energy away from reproductive behavior?

The starting point in understanding this whole matter lies in the potential function/s of sex. We often assume that sex is strictly for reproduction, but is this really true? Assuming that you have been reasonably sexually active, the number of times that you have had intercourse leading to reproduction, is likely insignificant compared to the total times that you have engaged in sex. To place a percent on this, let us take a person who has intercourse twice a week on average for ten years, for a total of 1040 times. If this individual has 2 children then the percent of times for reproduction is a fraction of one percent! Such a low percentage for any activity does not constitute a major reason. For example, you walk to visit a particular friend a similar percent of the time. I doubt you would cite this as a major reason why you walk somewhere. When we consider that many people have no children, or maybe one throughout their entire life, then there are only two real options, first, that almost no one has sex, or second, that sex rarely leads to reproduction. Clearly the latter explanation wins the day given that sex is alive and well. Some of you might be thinking that if not for contraception, then the number of times intercourse leads to reproduction would increase. True, but the very fact that people take steps to ensure adequate contraception reinforces the perspective that sex, even in the form of intercourse, is not primarily for reproduction.

We must then shake the notion that sex is strictly for reproduction and look for other options. With this in mind we have to consider sexual activity more generally across species. As presented in the Animal "Homosexuality" chapter, we are far from being alone in engaging in homoerotic behavior, with such behavior seemingly the norm, and not the exception, given that it occurs in insects, invertebrates, reptiles, fish, birds, mammals, and primates. Since homoerotic behavior cannot, at least directly, lead to reproduction there has to be other reasons why people and animals engage in homoerotic behavior and sex more generally. As a starting point we have to think of what sexual behavior entails beyond the salient sexual act—At its most basic level sex simply facilitates non-aggressive contact between members of the same species. Members of different species interact typically via predator-prey relationships or symbiosis. When a wolf attacks deer the two species are interacting, with the wolf predator and the deer prey, as are sharks when they eat other fish. Symbiosis refers to instances where there is a mutually beneficial relationship between different species.

While predator-prey relationships are highly salient leading to the perception that they are more common, symbiosis is at least as common, demonstrating that nature is not all about violence. In the marine world many species engage in symbiosis, such as with anemones and anemonefish, including clownfish like the fictional Nemo. Anemonefish receive protection within the stinging tentacles of the anemone, and are immune to the toxins themselves. The anemone also receives protection because anemonefish chase away predators that can feed on their host. Many species of fish including rays and sharks are cleaned of parasites by cleaner fish and shrimps. There are even cleaning stations, much like our car washes, where fish go to be cleaned of parasites. Cleaner fish, such as small wrasses and certain shrimp species, sit waiting at these stations. Shrimps like Pederson's cleaning shrimp, will even wave their antennae to signal that the service is offered at the particular location. Cleaner fish and shrimp enter the mouth and gills of much larger carnivorous fish, with the latter refraining from eating them. The advantage of being cleaned of parasites apparently outweighs the opportunity for an easy meal.

As humans we might consider ourselves above such an arrangement, but consider that bacteria within each of us outnumber our own cells by a ratio of 10:1.

100

Symbiosis characterizes the relationship—We provide a home and nutrients for them, and they fulfill invaluable functions for us. For example, bacteria in our gastrointestinal track break down the complex carbohydrates found in many plants, transforming them into simpler and easily digested sugars. These bacteria are actually key players in regulating our internal environment. For instance, H. Pylori actually adjusts stomach acid such that the level is suitable to both itself and us. If the acid level is too high strains with a gene called cagA start producing proteins that signal the stomach to reduce the flow of acid. In some individuals cagA can promote ulcers, but for most of us it helps regulate acidity levels protecting against ulcers. Gut bacteria also provide us with vitamin B12 essential for cellular energy production, DNA synthesis, and the manufacture of fatty acids. It is only bacteria that can synthesize the enzymes required to form this vitamin. Without the assistance of gut bacteria we would simply not survive. So much for us humans being above nature.

Although predator-prey relationships and symbiosis explain how different species interact with each other, the same reasons do not apply to how members of a given species relate to each other—They usually do not do so via predator-prey relationships, and since they are essentially identical symbiosis does not seem to work either. Sexual contact provides a mostly non-aggressive way to interact that is often pleasurable. Indeed, sexual contact is one of the main forms of non-aggressive interaction that members of most species engage in. For example, many primates such as chimpanzees and the related bonobos, regularly engage in sexual activity with various individuals.

The benefits of sexual contact need not be restricted to other-sex members, given that the purpose is not simply for reproduction. Based on animal studies (see the Animal "Homosexuality" chapter) various functions of homoerotic behavior have been noted including:

-Proceptivity enhancement, meaning that homoerotic stimulation assists the individual in heteroerotic sex.

-Receptivity reduction whereby the stimulated partner wastes sexual energy, leaving more reproductive opportunities for the initiator of this strategy.

-Greater success in defending a nest or territory, necessary for successful rearing of offspring.

-Expression of sexual receptivity in females.

-Dominance assertion involving the communicating of dominant-submissive relationship standing.

-Practice for heterosexual copulation.

-Tension reduction.

-Reconciliation.

-Alliance formation.

The task is to try and determine the function/s that apply to humans.

A useful model for understanding human sexual behavior consists of primates given their related evolution. In trying to determine the function, or functions, of homoerotic behavior in primates, Paul Vasey reviewed behavioral studies in various primate species— Homosexual behavior in primates: A review of evidence and theory, published in the International Journal of Primatology in 1995. He examined a number of assumptions, theories, and research results pertaining to homosexuality in primate species to clarify what can often be a confusing picture. His synthesis of diverse information reveals the probable functions of primate homoerotic behavior. Let us look at each of the possibilities.

102

Proceptivity Enhancement and Receptivity Reduction:

Both of these explanations for homoerotic behavior were proposed to account for female-female mounting. In the case of proceptivity enhancement, female mounting mimicking the sexual behavior of males attracts dominant male partners, increasing the chances of the mounted female being inseminated. The mounting female does not gain any direct reproductive advantage, but gains either by reciprocal altruism having the favor returned to her by the other female at a later date, or kin selection—An individual's genes can be passed on in his or her own offspring, or by assisting the reproduction of those sharing the same genes (kin selection). The latter rationale for proceptivity enhancement requires that the two females share many genes, and hence are somewhat related. Receptivity reduction is not at all altruistic, with the mounting female reducing the receptivity of her mounted partner by providing alternative sexual stimulation.

Shared and unshared predictions follow from these two possible explanations for female homoerotic behavior. Both predict that the homoerotic behavior should only occur in the presence of males, and only when females are fertile. In the absence of these conditions there is no point to the behavior, at least from the perspective of these two explanations. Proceptivity enhancement further predicts that females should cease the homoerotic behavior once sexually motivated males arrive. The receptivity reduction hypothesis suggests that females should not solicit other females to mount them, given the sexual stimulation and satisfaction by the first mounting female.

The predictions made by both explanations have been tested in various primate species and the results do not support either. For example, with gray langurs such behavior definitely occurs out of sight of males, and with Japanese macaques females actually attempt to spatially and visually separate themselves from the group before engaging in female-female mounting. In addition, female-female mounting occurs quite frequently, and not just when the individual is fertile. Inconsistent with the proceptivity enhancement hypothesis, males appear disinterested when they encounter female-female mounting, and the females often ignore or threaten any male that does solicit them. Countering the receptivity reduction hypothesis is the observation that female gray langurs and Japanese macaques, actively solicit other females to mount them. Hence, at least as far as primates are concerned, there is no support for the proceptivity enhancement and receptivity reduction explanations for homoerotic behavior. For the most part proceptivity enhancement and receptivity reduction apply to cognitively simpler organisms such as reptiles.

Dominance Assertion Hypothesis:

This hypothesis is very frequently used to explain homoerotic interactions in primates. It specifies that these interactions reinforce dominance hierarchies, thereby reducing aggression. Research indicates that while some primate homoerotic behavior can be interpreted in this way, the situation is much more complicated. Numerous studies covering various primate species reveal that although dominant individuals, both male and female, mount more often, the mounting of a dominant by a subordinate same-sex individual is also quite common. Some studies demonstrate that subordinates mount dominant individuals after aggressive displays, the exact opposite to what is predicted by dominance assertion— Mounting by dominant individuals to solidify rankings should follow aggressive encounters. In addition, it has been observed in some instances that when dominant individuals mount subordinates affectionate behavior, and not aggression, is expressed. Further casting doubt on this explanation for primate homoerotic behavior, several studies show absolutely no relationship between rank and mounting behavior. If the dominance assertion hypothesis is valid, then there should be a very clear pattern of more dominant individuals mounting subordinates. The lack of clarity suggests that at best this explanation only accounts for limited instances of primate homoerotic behavior, perhaps pertaining to when individuals are engaging in "dominance negotiations."

Practice For Heterosexual Sex:

In certain primate species mounting behavior during the immature play phase does appear to be essential for competent successful reproduction when mature, but the sex of immature mounting does not seem to make a difference. The lack of selectivity detracts somewhat from this explanation for homoerotic behavior, given that heteroerotic and homoerotic play behavior both work, but yet does provide a rationale for some homoerotic behavior. However, in several species practice is not essential for successful adult reproductive behavior.

Moreover, with age homoerotic behavior occurs in contexts other than play, suggesting something different than a preparatory role. Hence, although homoerotic play behavior during the immature phase can serve as practice for later heteroerotic sex, the hypothesis does not account for adult homoerotic sex, and is not essential for later reproductive behavior, given that early heteroerotic play behavior suffices in those species requiring early life sexual practice.

Tension-Regulation Hypothesis:

Studies of several primate species support a relationship between homoerotic behavior and social tension regulation, in that social tension is often reduced via such behavior. For example, with bonobos social tensions often arise related to food, and it has been noted that homoerotic contact reduces this tension. More food is actually acquired by engaging in homoerotic sex when individuals enter a food patch. The frequency of genital to genital rubbing by females increases with the size of the food patch, the size presumed to reflect the amount of time they are close to each other, and hence the overall tension level. Amongst yellow baboons, southern pig-tailed macaques, and Celebes crested macacaques, homoerotic behavior has been found to increase inter-individual tolerance and reduce aggression during periods of tension and excitement. Vasey believes that the evidence definitely supports tension reduction as a motivation for homoerotic behavior in primates. It is important to note that bonobos as great apes are quite closely related to humans, and baboons have a troop social structure similar to our ancestor's hunting-gathering form of social organization. The presence of homoerotic-based social tension reduction in these species, then quite strongly supports the notion that it might also play a role in human homoerotic behavior.

Reconciliation Hypothesis:

Aggression between members of a given species is a common occurrence. What is often less visible, but equally powerful, is how conflicts are reconciled. The so-called reconciliation hypothesis presented by de Waal, predicts that individuals try to undo the social damage inflicted by aggression, and hence actively seek contact with former opponents. For instance, preschool children seem to naturally display two forms of reconciliation— Peaceful associative outcomes in which both opponents stay together and work things out on the spot, and friendly reunions between opponents after temporary distancing. In addition to decreasing aggression, these two forms of reconciliation have been found to diminish stress related agitation, while increasing tolerance. Specific conciliatory behaviors engaged in by preschoolers include, play invitations, body contacts, verbal apologies, object offerings, and self-ridicule. As it pertains to adults, the reconciliation hypothesis might explain why families that are closest sometimes fight the most—They have more effective ways of repairing damage to relationships within the family. It might also account for the common occurrence of couples making love after an argument.

Studies of nonhuman primates have examined the frequency of attractions and dispersals following conflict. These studies have almost universally shown that opponents systematically contact each other more often than expected, supporting the reconciliation hypothesis. Reconciliation can involve different behaviors depending on the species including, kissing, embracing, sexual intercourse, clasping the other's hips, grooming, grunting, and holding hands. Evidence also indicates that the chance of renewed aggression is reduced and tolerance restored after reconciliation. Third parties can be involved in the reconciliation process and three patterns have been identified in this regard consisting of: Policing and pacification, triadic reconciliation, and third-party mediation. Policing and pacification involves a high-ranking member of the group intervening to reduce tensions. Triadic reconciliation consists of relatives of the victim seeking contact with the opponent. For example, with macaque and vervet monkeys relatives of the victim may approach and groom the attacker. Third-party mediation is the most complex variant, and so far has only been seen with chimpanzees, where a female will sometimes act as a catalyst by bringing rival males together.

Regarding homoerotic behavior de Waal has found that bonobos use it to reestablish bonds following aggressive encounters. For example, homoerotic mounts increase significantly in the 15-minute period after conflicts related to food. The aggressor is more likely to initiate homoerotic contact suggesting that this individual is attempting to resolve the conflict. Homoerotic behavior between female bonobos can even end aggression encounters in mid stride. Homoerotic reconciliation has also been noted with southern pig-tailed macaques and Celebus crested macaques. Homoerotic behavior for the purpose of reconciliation then definitely applies to at least some primate species.

Alliance Formation Hypothesis:

Fairbanks and colleagues in 1977 were the first to suggest that homoerotic behavior can assist with alliance formation. Observing rhesus macaques in an experimental situation, they noted high levels of homoerotic behavior between females in newly formed groups containing many unfamiliar individuals. They state, "The females who could form the first bonds joined in coalitions against their undefended peers and attempted to drive them from the group. This division of the social group into "bonded females" and "strangers" was apparently the first stage in the formation of a new group." While this observation might be attributed to the artificial experimental situation, several free-ranging primate species show homoerotic behavior during intergroup contact and transfer between groups, both circumstances involving social instability where alliance formation is adaptive.

Alliance formation also appears to be a major motivation for homoerotic behavior in primates during periods of social stability. For example, unrelated female Japanese macaques form stable bonds via homoerotic behavior, providing an additional source of social support above and beyond kin relations. There also appears to be a very important status augmentation role for the least socially dominate member of the pair, as evidenced by subordinate Japanese macaque females outranking all individuals between themselves and their dominate partners, so long as the homoerotic alliance remains intact. Support for homoerotic alliance formation also occurs with males. For example, male yellow baboons that mount and manipulate each other's genitalia form the most cohesive and successful alliances against other males. The frequency of homoerotic behavior increases prior to challenging a rival in order to reaffirm their alliance bond. Demonstrating that the homoerotic behavior is mutual, and not due to the dominant animal forcing support from a subordinate, intensely bonded males encourage symmetry in their relationship, with each actively soliciting mounts and genital fondling.

The role of homoerotic relationships in alliance formation, for both females and males, is supported by research examining various primate species. For example, homoerotic behavior between female bonobos allows partners to monopolize food sources, deter male harassment, and even gain entrance into a new group. Male gelada baboons and gray langurs homoerotic-based alliances have been found to increase the success of attacks on resident males in a group. Amongst hamadryas baboons, homoerotic behavior has been linked to alliance formation, and that in turn to the acquisition of females. Homoerotic behavior can be quite extensive including mutual embracing, grooming, penis display, touching, oral stimulation and mounting.

Given the many benefits of homoerotic alliance formation, it follows that the process actually enhances survival and reproductive success. For example, subordinate baboon and rhesus males occupying perimeter positions, making them more vulnerable to attack, frequently form homoerotic connections not involving dominant-submissive displays. These relationships help ensure assistance in the event of an attack by a predator, or aggression by a more dominate male if an attempt is made to reproduce. More directly demonstrating an enhancement of evolutionary fitness, homoerotic behavior can actually increase access of subordinate males to reproductively active females. For example, sexual activity between peripheral males might stimulate increased testosterone that in combination with alliance formation leads to reproductive opportunities. Frequently, younger peripheral rhesus monkeys establish homoerotic relationships with more dominant established males, the former gaining social support and elevated dominance status, thereby increasing the chances of reproduction. Dominant males also gain support for both defensive and offensive interactions. The dominance status of lower ranking female monkeys, such as rhesus and Japanese macaques, has also been observed to be elevated when the individual forms a homoerotic alliance with a more socially dominant female. Elevated status and alliance formation means protection, resources, and reproductive access to the more dominant males of the group presumably possessing better quality genes.

Primate research then reveals various functions served by homoerotic behavior, beyond non-aggressive and sometimes pleasurable social contact. Vasey's review finds the strongest support for alliance formation, with solid supporting roles provided by tension reduction and reconciliation. These three roles are actually highly related in that they foster social solidarity. For instance, when there is conflict or points of friction homoerotic behavior can help reduce tension and reconcile differences. Alliance formation often prevents conflict between partners, and provides support when a challenge is launched against one of the pair. It also assists both partners in acquiring important resources by elevating their dominance as a united social unit. The lower-ranking member of the homoerotic partnership in particular stands to gain more resources, and of significance from an evolutionary fitness perspective, in some instances has access to reproductive partners that might otherwise not be possible without incurring attacks by higher-ranking members of the group. While the focus here is on the purpose/s of homoerotic behavior, these three functions also apply to heteroerotic behavior, because it can reduce tension, help reconcile conflicts, and strengthen the alliance between partners. However, heteroerotic contact can increase tension and conflict between competing same-sex individuals.

HUMAN HOMEROTIC BEHAVIOR:

Although the evidence is very strong that alliance formation and the related functions of tension reduction and reconciliation play a major role in primate homoerotic behavior, it does not prove that these functions apply to human homoerotic behavior. For that we must take a look at hunting-gathering groups, the historical record, and modern-day examples. A crucial investigation of these issues was conducted by Frank Muscarella and reported in his article, The evolution of homoerotic behavior in humans. Evidence indicates that human homoerotic behavior dates well back into prehistory, based on 17,000-year old Paleolithic cave paintings showing male erections connected. Although it is difficult to determine exactly what life in hunting-gathering groups was like for early humans, it is almost certain that competition existed for reproductively active females, and that the status a male held in the group influenced reproductive success. Social status was a function of political strength and alliances formed. Even today females are attracted to signs of higher status, such as expensive clothing, good grooming, valuable possessions, and a confident attitude. Conversely, cues indicating a low social status are more of a turn-off, and have to be well compensated for as with very attractive features. Female social status would also have been crucial, and higher status females would likely have had more access to higher status males.

Social status and political standing within the group were undoubtedly influenced by age, in that older mature individuals had more chance to develop the knowledge, skills, experience, and alliances required to achieve a higher status. On the lowest end of the social status spectrum were those just entering puberty, with limited knowledge, skills, experience, and alliances with adults. Children not yet achieving reproductive capacity were likely removed from the social status game, and hence relatively sheltered from it. Entering puberty and becoming reproductively active appears to have entailed a shift to a low status position in the competitive social hierarchy. How might an individual in this position best manage the situation? One very solid option was to form alliances with higher-ranking individuals. Given that competition largely focuses on reproduction, alliances with other-sex members would not work. Higher-ranking same-sex individuals would likely punish the individual and restore the social order. Hence, the only real option was alliances with higher-ranking same-sex individuals. As with many primate species these alliances were probably based largely on sexual contact, the pleasurable nature of it communicating positive intentions and feelings, in contrast to aggression.

The historical record, and even modern day hunting-gathering group examples, suggests that alliances based on sexual contact between young low-ranking members of the social group and higher-ranking older same-sex individuals were a frequent occurrence. Often, at least for males, this starts during initiation rites into puberty. For instance, amongst the Sambia of highland New Guinea, puberty initiation rites for boys involve sexual contact, typically of an oral nature, with older more established men of the group. These alliances can persist for a decade or so, and then the younger men enter into relationships with females and produce children. There does not appear to be any difficulty in their engaging in these homoerotic acts, and then later shifting to predominately heteroerotic behavior. Interestingly, approximately 10-20% of South Pacific cultures approve of homoerotic relationships between young and older individuals. To those lacking insight into the important alliance formation aspect of these sexual unions, the occurrence of such behavior might induce a sense of moral disgust, but an awareness of how important alliances between young and older same-sex individuals have been throughout our evolution, can dispel these negative feelings and replace them with understanding.

Evidence from diverse cultures support the alliance formation role of homoerotic relationships, and in particular those involving low-ranking younger individuals and higher-ranking more mature members of society. In the Iliad the relationship between low status Patroclus and high-ranking Achilles is described. Patroclus is a marginalized member of a foreign group, after fleeing his own group to avoid punishment for a murder he committed. The relationship with Achilles, that is understood to be sexual, allows him to achieve a high rank and reproductive opportunities, because Achilles gives him access to female captives accorded him due to his acquired high status. Without the homoerotic alliance with Achilles, Patroclus might not even have survived, let alone have access to females. Similar alliances with reproductive opportunities have also been noted in all-male pirate societies, and other criminal organizations through the centuries. The image portrayed by various media of macho and straight men in these settings is then far from the truth, other than perhaps for the macho part.

Indeed homoerotic alliances between young low status males and older higher status men are recorded amongst Melanesian, Australian Aboriginal, Thai, Chinese, Japanese, Roman, and Greek societies. The younger men gain by elevating their social status without putting in all the work often necessary to do so. With higher status comes preferential access to important resources, and of particular significance from an evolutionary fitness perspective, access to reproductive age females. In some instances the females accessed are also of higher rank in the group, adding further to the advantages of homoerotic alliance formation with older higher status males. Hence, homoerotic-based alliance formation ironically led to increased heteroerotic success for the younger lower-ranking member of the partnership! You might be wondering what the older higher-ranking male of the group gets from the deal? In addition to sexual stimulation, there is support in the event of any challenge from another male of the group. In such an instance having a young, healthy, and strong male ally could prove very useful. As the older individual ages, he might even hold onto a higher status position by virtue of his alliance with a younger partner who is advancing in strength and status.

Does the same process apply to females? Evidence suggests that it does, but details are less clear due to the greater emphasis on recording male events throughout history. However, homoerotic-based relationships between females were present in ancient Chinese, Greek, Roman, and numerous other civilizations. These unions seem to foster alliances and reduce social tensions. Amongst present day Mombasa people of Kenya, homoerotic alliances between older wealthier women and young poor women are quite common. Co-wives in polygynous societies of Africa also commonly partake in homoerotic relationships. These relationships might well reduce social tensions that can easily arise when there are co-wives, and ensure support if required. As with non-human primates, human female homoerotic behavior appears to have aided in alliance formation providing protection, resources, and mating opportunities with higher-ranking male members of the society.

One crucial implication of the alliance formation function of homoerotic behavior, is that those who have a zero or very low motivation on the homoerotic dimension might well have been at a disadvantage throughout evolution, based on an inability to form fitness enhancing alliances with same-sex members of the group or society. Considering that the heteroerotic dimension is separate, a solid homoerotic motivation would not have precluded reproduction. In contrast, it appears to have enhanced opportunities to capitalize on heteroerotic motivation. This rationale can be extended further in that a very high heteroerotic motivation, combined with an extremely low homoerotic motivation, could have resulted in attacks and ostracism both reducing reproductive opportunities— Individuals with this combination might have sought reproductive opportunities without alliance support, incurring the wrath of higher-ranking members of the group. This wrath could entail physical attacks producing injury or death, or ostracism involving diminished access to important resources or rejection from the group. Some degree of homoerotic motivation would help ensure sufficient alliance formation, reducing the likelihood of fitness diminishing ostracism.

A common feature of homoerotic alliances is an age differential, consisting of an older higher status individual forming a relationship with a younger lower status member of the group. Interestingly, a similar process is quite common in heteroerotic relationships, with older

116

higher-ranking males forming relationships with younger lower-ranking females. These alliances are particularly common when resources are hard to come by and disproportionately allocated. The older higher-ranking male acquires a solid reproductive opportunity and other benefits derived from a youthful partner, while the female acquires resources that can ensure her survival and that of her offspring. In addition, the success of her partner indicates the possibility of superior genes.

Due to the evolutionary fitness enhancing benefits of both heteroerotic and homoerotic behavior, each person inherits a capacity for both, taking the form of a specific level or small range of motivation for each. This arrangement occurs because much like personality dimensions, the value of a given level of heteroerotic and homoerotic motivation varies with social and environmental circumstances. For instance, if during our evolution few reproductively active females were present and competition for them intense, a higher homoerotic and more moderate level heteroerotic motivation in males might be most adaptive—This combination fosters alliances that could facilitate reproductive opportunities, provides sufficient motivation to take advantage of these opportunities, but not so much that the male skips alliance formation and prematurely seeks mating opportunities, resulting in attacks and ostracism from more dominant men. Conversely, in a setting with many reproductively active females and little competition, a higher heteroerotic motivation and lower homoerotic motivation might be more adaptive, because homoerotic alliance formation would not be as important. For females a similar pattern would apply, but the emphasis would be on higher quality males for reproduction given limits to reproductive capacity (the likely number of offspring that a typical woman can have).

As it turns out then, homoerotic behavior serves several important functions, and actually enhances reproductive success! Hence, the so-called evolutionary or Darwinian paradox is no paradox at all. Homoerotic behavior fosters same-sex alliance formation, while also providing a mechanism to reduce social tensions and reconcile conflicts and aggressive encounters. These roles promote social stability and improve the odds of survival. Homoerotic alliances during our evolution, and even in more recent times, appear to have helped younger lower-ranking members of society rise in status and secure reproductive opportunities, and certainly with higher-ranking individuals, thereby providing a clear evolutionary fitness benefit. In addition, it turns out that the value of a given level of homoerotic motivation varies with social environmental circumstances accounting for the range of such behavior, and why people differ in their level of homoerotic motivation. The strength of this perspective on homoerotic behavior derives first, from how it resolves the evolutionary paradox and, second, that it provides us with an enlightened understanding that should greatly reduce negativity towards those perceived as not being straight—Persecution is much less likely to occur if the persecutor realizes that they also have some capacity for the targeted behavior. Given how common homoerotic behavior appears to have been throughout evolution, and how if anything it actually has enhanced reproductive success, it even appears that we all have some non-zero level of homoerotic motivation.

It might be suggested that the perspective presented regarding homoerotic and heteroerotic behavior, only represents a hypothesized evolutionary mechanism vulnerable to creative interpretation. However, considering first, the widespread presence of these two dimensions in very diverse animal species, second, clear-cut functions served by them, third, the evidence for alliance formation, reconciliation, and tension reduction in primates, fourth, the apparent adaptive nature of these functions applied to humans, thereby satisfying a high threshold for any postulated evolutionary function, and fifth, the impracticalities associated with a single dimension of sexual orientation, it is reasonable to assume that homoerotic and heteroerotic dimensions exist in humans, likely serving at least the functions of alliance formation, reconciliation, and tension reduction. Additional value might be derived simply from pleasure and sexual release.

Some of you might be wondering what this perspective has to say about homosexuality. Is there anything that actually corresponds to homosexuality? We all have homoerotic and heteroerotic dimensions that are inherited, and as such neurologically based. In addition, due to the need to reproduce the value on the heteroerotic dimension is almost certainly non-zero, providing at least some capacity to reproduce. Virtually all "gay" men are capable of having intercourse at least once to procreate, it is just that they are not highly motivated and will not relish the experience. "Lesbians" can and often have engaged in intercourse with men, although they do not really enjoy it. Likewise, it appears that we all have a non-zero level of homoerotic motivation, providing the capacity to form same-sex alliances when the need arises, and to reduce social tensions and reconcile conflicts. A low heteroerotic motivation and high homoerotic motivation corresponds to being "homosexual," much as a high heteroerotic and low homoerotic motivation aligns with being a "heterosexual." However, despite the popularity of these designations, "homosexuality" and "heterosexuality" are not real entities, but just descriptions of natural occurrences—Homoerotic and heteroerotic dimensions.

Another question pertains to why most people identify with being heterosexual and relatively few with homosexuality or bisexuality. The matter of sexual orientation identification is a crucial one and will be explored in the chapters that follow, particularly the social construction one. What can be presented at this point, though, is that given the importance of reproduction to evolutionary fitness and the direct role that the heteroerotic dimension plays in reproduction, it is highly likely that heteroerotic motivation is substantially larger than homoerotic motivation on average, meaning that people will naturally tend to have a higher level on the heteroerotic dimension than the homoerotic one. Due to this occurrence most people will identify with being heterosexual. Since only a minority of people will have a stronger homoerotic motivation than heteroerotic motivation, or approximately equal levels of both, a minority of people will identify with being homosexual or bisexual, respectively. Before exploring other aspects of sexual orientation identification we have to examine the crucial and novel topic of homoerotic and heteroerotic dimension activation.

HOMOEROTIC & HETEROEROTIC DIMENSION ACTIVATION

We have seen how sexuality in humans and other animals works by dimensions. The concept of dimensions at first glance suggests something that is present or absent, and that is about it. We have the capacity or we do not. However, there is a crucial component that is almost always missed even by experienced researchers—Dimensions can be inactive or active, and even active to varying degrees! To take a simple example, let's assume that you are interested in listening to music. When working you might not even remotely be thinking about music, but the sound of a song you like piques your interest and you turn on your own radio. A way of conceptualizing this occurrence is that your interest in music was not activated in the process of doing your work, but became active upon hearing the song. We can go even further and say that your fondness for the song strongly activated your interest in music. This process aligns with how the brain, and body more generally, tends to be structured on the basis of activation and deactivation in response to circumstances. For example, visual sensory input activates the occipital lobe of the brain responsible for processing visual information, and the presence of pathogens within the body typically activates genes that ramp up immune system responses.

The concept of dimension activation applies well to Costa and MacCrea's "Big 5" personality dimensions—Introversion/extroversion, emotional reactivity, openness to experience, conscientiousness, and agreeableness. With introversion/extroversion, unique or new social scenarios can activate the dimension and a person's level is expressed. As an example, when out with a friend you end up at a party that your companion was invited to. The highly social nature of this experience is clearly relevant to introversion/extroversion. Consequently, the dimension is activated and your natural proclivity for such experiences comes out. If you are the proverbial life of the party, meaning high in extroversion, you warm up to the opportunity and readily engage in conversation. On the other hand, if you are more to the introverted end of the spectrum, a feeling of apprehension or even dread is likely to arise limiting social interactions. Perhaps you even make an excuse to leave within the hour. If your level of introversion/extroversion is somewhere in the mid range you might show social behavior between these two extremes, and be more influenced by the atmosphere. When it is warm and inviting you will engage quite well, but if cold and aloof then you will shrink back. You might even indulge in excess alcohol to settle your negative feelings, and become more extroverted than what comes natural.

The emotional reactivity dimension tends to be activated when circumstances change abruptly. For instance, you are sitting at your desk working and your boss shouts. This abrupt change automatically triggers a response, the intensity consistent with your natural level on the reactivity dimension. If you are to the reactive end your likely thoughts will be something like, "Oh no, she's upset with me, I must have done something wrong!" However, if you are to the low end of the reactivity dimension you might wonder, "What's bothering her?" In the former instance you start fidgeting anticipating your boss marching to your desk, whereas in the latter you refocus on your work. The emotional reactivity dimension has been activated and your natural level expressed by the abrupt change. Novel circumstances activate the openness to experience dimension. For example, you win a free sky diving lesson in a raffle. If you are very open to experience the win is savored and you try it out. On the other hand, if you are closed to experience you will instantly feel like pulling back and rejecting the opportunity, maybe passing the winning ticket to a more adventurous friend.

The dimension of conscientiousness is activated whenever a task presents itself. Those high on this personality variable are motivated to engage and see it through to completion, while those low in conscientiousness are likely to avoid it or do the minimum required. Social contact particularly involving verbal communication activates the agreeableness dimension. Another person makes a comment regarding a politician. If you are high on the agreeable dimension you will automatically think of a way to align viewpoints. If you are more to the disagreeable end of the dimension you will take the devils' advocate position and come across as contrary, and even argumentative. Hence, dimensions of personality are activated by circumstances relevant to the given dimension, and once the dimension is activated a person's natural level is expressed. Over time a person's level on each of these personality dimensions can and does change. Earlier research suggested that everyone has a fixed point on the "Big 5" that never varies. It is now appreciated that levels do change over time. For example, throughout adulthood people typically become more extroverted and conscientious, and less reactive, with openness to experience and extroversion declining somewhat in very old age. A person's natural level then shifts with time and environmental influences. Of course those higher on the given dimension will engage in experiences consistent with their motivation, such as a person who is more open to experience partaking in adventurous activities, or a person higher in extroversion seeking social contact. These experiences will in turn further activate that given personality dimension, leading to enhanced behavior of the particular type.

Much like personality dimensions, sexual dimensions can be activated, and to varying degrees, by circumstances. Take for example the "masculinity" and "femininity" dimensions, with aggression and nurturing behavior, respectively. Both behaviors are frequently required due to social and environmental circumstances. During our evolution attacks by predators and competing hunting-gathering groups necessitated an aggressive defense. Our lack of body weaponry compared to many other animals meant that we often needed an even greater level of aggression, expressed by shouting, arm waving, throwing objects, and actual attack behavior aided by numbers and weapons. Whenever a danger was detected the "masculine" dimension, or the component relevant to aggression, became activated for both males and females. Aggression consistent with a person's naturally endowed motivation level would be expressed. A male low on this dimension would tend to act passively withdrawing from the situation, while a female high on it engaged aggressively.

In our ancestral hunting-gathering past, children required a lot of protection and assistance. The presence of children, and in particular those viewed as your own, activates the "feminine" dimension, or the nurturing component. A person's natural propensity for nurturing behavior is then expressed. A male with a high degree would tend to the child, while a female with low motivation would show less caring and assistance. Aggression and nurturing behavior are organized as

124

separate dimensions, reflecting a range of capacity for both. They are not on the same dimension as we have seen, because if so higher levels of aggression must mean lower levels of nurturance, and the converse with higher nurturance, scenarios that are invalid given that a person can have varying degrees of both capacities. We categorize the aggressive dimension as "masculine" and the nurturing as "feminine." Given their adaptive value during our evolution, the masculine and feminine dimensions, facilitating aggression and nurturing behavior, respectively, are indeed very much a part of all of us. There are of course other aspects to masculinity and femininity, as we learned in the Dimensions Of Sexual Orientation chapter, but aggression and nurturing behavior stand out because they have clear roles in our evolution.

At this point some of you might be thinking that aggression and nurturing behavior do not simply reflect a person's genetically encoded level. There is the matter of learned behaviors, for example. This is a very true comment and patterns of behavior evidenced by caregivers do have a major influence on whether or not, and to what extent, a person engages in aggression and nurturing behavior. If caregivers display a lot of anger and are physically abusive, a child learns the aggressive pattern of behavior and tends to repeat it despite having suffered from it. This is a key reason why child abuse tends to pass from one generation to the next. To end the transmission someone has to "break the cycle," and resist the learned tendency to act aggressively. In a similar fashion, if caregivers express a lot of nurturing behavior hugging and cuddling, that pattern of behavior is learned and repeated. If caregivers are cold and aloof showing little or no nurturing behavior, then the child tends to be socially distant and not caring.

How might the concept of dimension activation be reconciled with learned patterns of behavior? One way is to consider the impact of modeled behavior on dimension activation and deactivation—Dimensions consistent with a learned pattern of behavior are activated, while inconsistent ones are deactivated. Hence, when caregivers demonstrate an aggressive pattern of behavior, the "masculine" aggressive dimension is activated in an ongoing fashion. An individual's level of aggression emerges, with those low in it acting only slightly aggressively, and those high on it being bullies and the like. If the aggressive caregiver pattern is dominant and does not alternate with nurturing behavior, then the "feminine" dimension will be less activated or remain deactivated. Consequently, even if the person has a high level of nurturing capacity it will not be expressed, or to a lesser degree. Likewise, if a person sees and experiences a lot of nurturing behavior and little or no aggression, the "feminine" nurturing dimension will be activated ongoing, and the "masculine" aggressive dimension deactivated. The person's level of nurturing capacity will then emerge, but their motivation for aggression will not or to a lesser extent. If both aggressive and nurturing patterns of behavior are demonstrated by caregivers, then both dimensions can be activated, but perhaps not in such an ongoing fashion as when an aggressive or nurturing pattern dominates.

Learned patterns of behavior can also maximize a person's expressed level of behavior consistent with the activated dimension. This might best be conceptualized as strong activation of the relevant dimension. We probably inherit a small range for aggression and nurturing behavior, representing our natural propensity for actions of this type. The range encompasses threshold for expressing the behavior, intensity, duration, and how easy it is for the person to terminate the behavior. For example, if a person has a mild level of motivation for aggression that individual requires more stimulation to engage in attack behavior, it often is not that intense, does not last long, and can be more easily terminated. If a person has a high level, then aggression comes on fast, is extreme, of relatively long duration, and does not shut off easily. Exposure to an aggressive model strongly activates the masculine dimension, ensuring that the maximum value on the individual's aggression range is expressed.

The level of aggression can even extend beyond the natural range due to reinforcement effects. For instance, a child who naturally has a fairly low level of aggression, even at the maximum point on his or her range, starts to bully weaker kids and is reinforced by the money he gets from them. The level of expressed aggression then escalates beyond the maximum level that comes naturally, and over time the natural range recalibrates to a higher level. Nurturing behavior can be altered in a similar fashion—Via reinforcement effects the degree of nurturing behavior can shift beyond the highest point on the person's natural range. For example, having a child cuddle you in response to nurturing actions strongly reinforces those actions. With repeated reinforcement the person's natural range of nurturing behavior shifts to a higher level. Reinforcement for non-aggression or for non-nurturing behavior can likewise reduce a person's natural range on these two dimensions.

Various other aspects of masculinity and femininity can also be activated, such as mannerisms. A man who identifies with being "homosexual" might experience activation of the feminine dimension and express effeminate mannerisms. If the effeminate mannerisms are reinforced by positive attention, then activation of this aspect of femininity will be maintained and intensified.

127

However, if effeminate mannerisms are punished, such as when a "gay" man works in a traditionally masculine occupation, the feminine dimension, or at least this aspect of it, will be suppressed or deactivated, resulting in the expression of exclusively masculine mannerisms. A woman identifying as "homosexual" might experience activation of the masculine dimension, and express traditionally masculine mannerisms and other behaviors. If reinforced these mannerisms will become more prominent, but might recede or vanish if there is punishment. Activation of the masculinity and femininity dimensions and reinforcement of such behavior provides at least a partial explanation for why some "gay" men show effeminate behavior, and why some "lesbian" women demonstrate masculine behavior.

HOMOEROTIC & HETEROEROTIC DIMENSIONS:

Much like with the masculinity and femininity dimensions, the homoerotic and heteroerotic dimensions can be activated, and to varying degrees. The dominant dimension is preferentially active (heteroerotic in "heterosexuals" and homoerotic in "homosexuals"), but the less dominant dimension can be activated by various influences. This is a fascinating process helping explain many puzzling aspects of human sexuality. One such aspect is the higher frequency of homoerotic activity in same-sex settings. For example, researchers such as Money, and also Bell and colleagues, have found that adolescent boys in same-sex boarding schools engage in more homoerotic behavior than boys in mixed-sex schools. The same phenomenon at all-female colleges is common, being referred to by Diamond as "lesbian until graduation." Homoerotic activity is also more common in other same-sex settings, such as prisons and nunneries. It might be suggested that many of those who engage in homoerotic behavior in same-sex settings are actually "gay," perhaps even being drawn in some instances to the setting due to their homosexual orientation. Of course this would not apply to prisons. Countering this notion is the reality that heteroerotic behavior frequently occurs when the individual shifts to mixed-sex settings. For instance, although adolescent boys in same-sex boarding schools quite commonly partake in homoerotic sex, they do not demonstrate higher rates of such behavior as adults. Male and female inmates fairly commonly engage in homoerotic sex, and certainly not always because they are forced to, but then often return to heteroerotic sex when they leave prison.

What is likely occurring in these instances of homoerotic behavior is that the same-sex setting is activating the homoerotic dimension, and certainly more than the heteroerotic dimension. Once the homoerotic dimension is activated, the individual's level of motivation is expressed. Even those with a fairly low motivation might be prompted to engage if there is sufficient motivation, such as the need for alliance formation or just affection. In prisons and conceivably same-sex schools having a trusted ally or allies, based on homoerotic contact, can be a valuable asset. Many people have survived emotionally and physically in prisons because of it. In female prisons women have been found to bond sexually, based on the need for friendship and a relationship that is supportive and not hostile, according to research by Maeve (The social construction of love and sexuality in a women's prison). The need for alliance formation might be seen as strongly activating a person's homoerotic dimension, ensuring that their maximal level of homoerotic motivation is expressed. Even the opportunity for sexual contact when heterosexual contact is not feasible, can activate the homoerotic dimension. Adolescent sex hormones might also strongly activate the homoerotic dimension in same-sex settings.

Reinforcement effects can actually push a person's motivation for homoerotic sex beyond their natural range. For example, if person is being bullied and a homoerotic alliance terminates the attacks, or results in the bully being beaten, then the homoerotic behavior might be so intensely reinforced that a person expresses a higher level than he or she is naturally motivated for. Upon leaving the same-sex setting activation of the homoerotic dimension ceases, in part due to the presence of other-sex individuals, and also how circumstances such as the need for same-sex alliance formation abruptly end. The presence of other-sex individuals activates the heteroerotic dimension, and the person's level of motivation for it is expressed.

Many other influences can activate the homoerotic and heteroerotic dimensions. For example, an affectionate touch by a same-sex individual can activate the homoeerotic dimension. Those with a higher level of motivation are more likely to respond favorably. A touch by an other-sex individual will activate the heteroerotic dimension, and the individual's level of motivation will be expressed. Some very interesting interpersonal dynamics play a role as evidenced by waiters/waitresses and customers. A female waitress touching a male tends to illicit better tips, whereas the other options—female waitress touching a female customer, male waiter touching a male customer, and male waiter touching a female customer—have much more variable results. A female waitress touching a male customer can activate the heteroerotic dimension, and quite strongly if the female is attractive. The male customer is unlikely to feel threatened, at least not by the waitress. His wife or girlfriend looking on might be another story, prompting him to contain his reaction. The man is motivated to give a good tip due to the pleasant activation of the heteroerotic dimension, assuming that he has a substantial level of motivation in this regard. His partner who has observed the touch and his response might suggest a lesser tip. If the man has a low level of heteroerotic motivation, then the touch will likely have little impact or even the reverse effect of irritation.

A female waitress touching a female customer, or male waiter touching a male customer, can activate the homoerotic dimension, but this might produce a feeling of embarrassment or fear, particularly since we do not seem to readily accept our homoerotic capacity if we identify with being heterosexual. These negative reactions might result in a poor tip, or at least one less ideal than without the physical contact. If a person is more accepting of their homoerotic motivation and has other than a very low level, then the touch is often responded to favorably resulting in a better tip. A male waiter touching a female customer might well activate the heteroerotic dimension, but this action might be perceived as intrusive and reacted to negatively, leaving the waiter with a poor tip. If the customer perceives that the touch is strictly a manipulation to get a better tip and not sincere, activation of the relevant dimension (heteroerotic for other-sex servers and homoerotic for same-sex servers) might be terminated resulting in a lesser tip. However, activation of these dimensions is such a powerful influence that even an awareness of manipulation might not suffice to deactivate them. So even a simple touch in a restaurant by a waiter or waitress can have a very significant impact on heteroerotic/homoerotic dimension activation, and strongly influence behavior.

The social dimensions—heterosocial and homosocial—might also play a role in this scenario, particularly given that a restaurant setting is not very sexual. Activation and deactivation of these dimensions can augment, counter, or compensate for activation/deactivation of the sexual orientation dimensions. So for example, if a female waitress touches a man who likes socializing with females (high heterosocial motivation) and who also has a high heteroerotic motivation, then activation of the heterosocial and heteroerotic dimensions will be additive. If on the other hand, he dislikes socializing with females (low heterosocial motivation), then the activated heteroerotic and heterosocial motivations might counter each other moderating the former influence. If a male waiter touches a male customer who has a high homosocial motivation (likes socializing with males) and a low homoerotic motivation, then the negative reaction based on the latter motivation might be compensated for by the high homosocial motivation.

Sexual orientation dimension activation can even account for seemingly unexplainable sexual occurrences. For example, a man lives a heterosexual life with wife and kids, but after the kids are grown up starts engaging in homoerotic behavior. In many instances the individual has suppressed his homoerotic motivation and led a "straight" life. In others the person has actually acted on the homoerotic motivation but done so in a secretive fashion, such as in bathhouses. Many "gay" men encounter numerous "straight" men in bathhouses and the like. However, in at least some instances the man does not appear to be aware of any significant homoerotic motivation until later in life, and then starts to act on it in

132

line with how sexual orientation and behavior does show flexible change over time. What is likely occurring in these instances is that, during his reproductive years the heterosexual dimension was activated and maintained by the presence of children and his sexually active wife, but when the children become adults and sexual relations with his wife slow, the homoerotic dimension starts to become activated. Perhaps there might be a trigger such as encountering a young attractive man.

The same type of process can apply to women, such as when a female who has a history of exclusive heteroerotic relationships enters into a homoerotic relationship. In this instance the homoerotic dimension is activated, with participation reflecting a significant homoerotic motivation. If this romance ends and a suitable male comes along, then the heteroerotic dimension is once again activated. Some individuals readily engage in homoerotic relationships upon entering into same-sex settings such as prison, but after leaving return to heteroerotic relationships. Their heteroerotic motivation is likely higher than their homoerotic motivation, with the former preferentially activated, but in the presence of same-sex individuals and the need for alliance formation or other benefits, the homoerotic dimension becomes activated. Conversely, there are instances of individuals identifying as homosexual forming a tight emotional bond with an other-sex person, and entering into a romantic relationship. The strength of the emotional bond likely activates the less dominant heteroerotic dimension, thereby accounting for the sexual relationship. An opportunity to reproduce can also activate the less dominant heteroerotic dimension, particularly if the opportunity is combined with emotional closeness to the other-sex person.

The concept of sexual orientation dimension activation/deactivation might also help account for why identical twins are only 20-50% concordant for sexual orientation (see the Biological Theories chapter). Aside from early environmental non-shared influences impacting on the level of homoerotic and heteroerotic motivation, it is feasible that alternative dimensions might be preferentially activated in each twin as development proceeds, perhaps as a way of establishing individual identities. This differential activation of sexual orientation dimensions takes the twins down different paths of sexual development helping to distinguish them.

It is often assumed that homosexuality involves gender atypical behavior, with males more effeminate and females more masculine. As we have seen, though, homosexual men are not necessarily effeminate and homosexual women masculine. It is a nice and simple stereotype that does not really apply that well. However, some researchers find a trend in this direction. One unique possibility that follows from sexual orientation dimension activation, is that feminine characteristics in males might enhance activation of the homoerotic dimension, resulting in increased behavior of this type, with the same scenario applying to females who have significant masculine characteristics. The presence of feminine characteristics in a male, and masculine characteristics in a female, might also attract more homoerotic partners. Females with strong masculine characteristics often report being seduced by homosexual women. Likewise, men with feminine characteristics often experience more sexual advances by homosexual men, based on the perception that they are homosexual. Activation of the homoerotic dimension, due to this sexual attention, might augment activation derived from the presence of feminine characteristics in males and masculine characteristics in females.

The puzzling and confusing impact of sexual abuse on the expression of sexual orientation, is also much more understandable when we consider homoerotic and heteroerotic dimension activation and deactivation. One of the fascinating aspects of sexual abuse is that it has variable and very difficult to explain effects on sexual orientation. In some instance the abused tends to engage in increased sexual behavior consistent with the sex of the abuser (homoerotic if same-sex and heteroerotic if other-sex), while in other instances there is less or no sexual behavior of this type, according to several researchers, such as Bramblett & Darling, Brown, Harrison, and McLaughlin. For example, Harrison and colleagues (The impact of prior heterosexual experiences on homosexuality in women) have found that lesbians report more severe and frequent sexual abuse by men, and at a younger age, than heterosexual women. The abuse appears to play a role in their expressed sexual orientation. This is not to say that sexual abuse causes sexual orientation. Instead, activation and deactivation of sexual orientation dimensions can account for these puzzling occurrences.

Sexual abuse, and particularly during an early sensitive period of development, can activate the sexual dimension corresponding to the sex of the perpetrator— The homoerotic dimension in the case of same-sex perpetrators and the heteroerotic dimension with other-sex perpetrators. This early and often repetitive activation of the given dimension can lead to overly sexualized behavior consistent with the activated dimension. For example, sexually abused young females often display overly sexualized behavior towards men, such behavior constituting one of the signs of sexual abuse. Likewise, a young male engaging in non-violent and stimulating sexual contact with an older male, will often express enhanced homoerotic behavior, such as actively soliciting peers for homoerotic relationships. Sexualization of behavior is one of the most consistently reported impacts of sexual abuse, as confirmed by researchers such as Calam and colleagues, Estes and Tidwell, Hotte and Rafman, and Putman. For example, Calam and colleagues followed 144 sexually abused children and adolescents for 2 years after the criminal investigation, and found that sexualized behavior increased over this time frame. Sexualization might be more likely to occur when sexual arousal is experienced, as discovered by Hall and colleagues (Factors associated with sexual behavior in young sexually abused children). Research by Middleton (Ongoing incestuous abuse during adulthood) has shown that sexual abuse involving close relatives maximizes sexualization of behavior, apparently due to sexualization of attachment. In contrast to what is commonly thought, those who perpetrate sexual abuse are often attentive to the needs of the abused, and are violent in only a minority of instances, according to research by Murray (Psychological profile of pedophiles and child molesters). This attentiveness is one reason why they often get away with it, and frequently over a prolonged period.

On the other hand, if sexual abuse is sufficiently traumatic then avoidance behavior often occurs, involving deactivation or suppression of the corresponding sexual dimension. Hence, a male violently abused by an older male might experience deactivation of the homoerotic dimension, and reject such behavior even if there is a substantial motivation for it. A female aggressively abused by a male likewise might experience deactivation of the heteroerotic dimension, making it more likely that the homoerotic dimension will become activated. If there is sufficient homoerotic motivation she will engage with females, but if not will appear asexual even though she might actually have a fairly solid heteroerotic motivation. Deactivation of a sexual orientation dimension due to traumatic abuse then has the effect of accentuating the alternative dimension, or contributing to asexuality if motivation for the alternative dimension is very low. The notion that sexual orientation dimensions can be activated or deactivated aligns with research indicating that homoerotic behavior can be triggered by circumstances, such as that conducted by Easpaig and colleagues, Iasenza, Kennedy, McKenzie, and Pedersen & Kristiansen. Paul and colleagues (Brain response to visual sexual stimuli in heterosexual and homosexual males) discovered that different brain regions are activated in response to sexual stimuli consistent and inconsistent with expressed sexual orientation, suggesting the possibility of a neural basis for homoerotic and heteroerotic dimension activation/deactivation.

A couple of case examples will help illustrate the impact of sexual abuse on sexual orientation. As a child Jane (not her real name) experienced sexual abuse by her alcoholic stepfather. The contact was not violent and indeed constituted the only affection he showed towards her. As a teenager she became promiscuous in a heteroerotic way, and later ended up being raped on one occasion when intoxicated. This turned her off heterorotic sex for some time, and she started to engage with female friends. The support that she felt from them reinforced this behavior, and she became almost exclusively "lesbian" for a number of years. Then after a painful breakup she met a "decent guy" and started into a romance with him. Homoerotic and heteroerotic dimension activation and deactivation can account for her behavior. The "affectionate" emotional contact from her stepfather during the sexual abuse highly activated her heteroerotic dimension, contributing to the excessive heteroerotic behavior as a teenager. The rape was traumatic and it resulted in a deactivation of her heteroerotic dimension, perhaps also due to reactivated and suppressed negative feelings arising from the sexual abuse by her stepfather. With her heteroerotic dimension deactivated her less intense homoerotic motivation was activated, and she engaged in several romances of this type. The painful breakup appeared to deactivate her homoerotic dimension, while the encounter with the decent man activated her heteroerotic dimension again.

Bob is a middle-age man who identifies as being "homosexual." He recalls his father sexually molesting him from a young age. He reported the fondling as somewhat stimulating, not an uncommon reaction, but the few times of anal penetration as being very frightening and painful. Sexual abuse of this severity is quite rare from biological fathers or mothers, and certainly in the absence of alcohol/drug abuse and/or severe psychiatric illness. When Bob was an adult he discovered via hidden records, that his father was not his biological father, nor for that matter was his mother his biological mother. His mother's sister had an "illegitimate" child, that if revealed during the mid-1950's era and location in a rural community would have been a major embarrassment. She was kept on the farm during the pregnancy and gave the child up to his parents, who were apparently having trouble conceiving. At the same time Bob's father experienced violent psychotic episodes, potentially related to brain damage from physical abuse by his own father. In addition, Bob's mother told him after his father's death that she always thought her husband was "gay." This information helps explain the sexual abuse Bob experienced.

As a young teenager Bob was attracted primarily to men, in part due to the early activation of his homoerotic dimension, although his natural level of homoerotic motivation certainly appears much greater than his heteroerotic motivation. He tried a few heteroerotic romances, but they did not really appeal to him. A very intriguing aspect of this story is that the types of sexual abuse he experienced as a child appear to have ironically saved his life. Bob "came out" in the late 1970's just before HIV and AIDS was on the scene. He describes himself as being very sexually active, but had zero motivation for anal sex. The painful experiences with his father had the effect of deactivating any homoerotic motivation when the possibility of anal sex arose. He would lose interest if a partner attempted it and exit the situation. However, oral and manual forms of homoerotic sex were both very stimulating for him, and he had numerous partners. Then as HIV and AIDS took hold his friends and partners began "dropping like flies" as he recounts. Bob remained free of the disease simply because he was turned off by the thought of anal sex, never engaging in it. If his father had not exacted this painful form of sexual abuse on him, he believes he would have died with all those other men. Yes, the twists and turns of life can be amazing.

As with personality dimensions and masculine and feminine dimensions, sexual orientation dimensions involve a natural range of motivation that can and frequently does shift over time. As Bob engaged in homoerotic experiences his motivation intensified for oral and manual sex, but his motivation for anal sex remained nil. Jane's heterorotic motivation intensified during her promiscuous teenage years, largely due to how reinforcing the behavior was in regards to getting attention from men, much as it gave her affection from her otherwise aloof stepfather. She recalls being very "popular" with men, not surprising given her receptivity. Her natural range of heteroerotic motivation shifted upwards, but then was deactivated and perhaps also decreased with the rape. As she engaged with women her homoerotic motivation increased.

Deactivation of sexual orientation dimensions, such as from sexual abuse, might account for an apparent zero motivation on one or both—Naturally there might be non-zero values to facilitate both homoerotic and heteroerotic behavior, but if a dimension is deactivated the person will appear to have no motivation at all. This is certainly conceivable in the case of sexual abuse and some forms of mental illness. For example, with severe depression a person loses motivation for many self-sustaining behaviors, and sexual functioning can be non-existent. The deficit state of schizophrenia consists of so-called absence symptoms, consisting of apathy, amotivation, avolition, anhedonia (absence of pleasure), motor retardation, affective blunting and absence of play and curiosity. Consequently, sexual motivation is absent in many of those with schizophrenia and so-called schizophrenic spectrum disorders. Perhaps then it is only in the context of sexual orientation dimension deactivation, due to sexual abuse or mental illness that zero motivation occurs providing for complete asexuality.

We started out our discussion of dimension activation/deactivation examining the analogy of personality dimensions. Linking personality and homoerotic/heteroerotic dimensions, people with a high level of motivation on the openness to experience dimension are probably more likely to activate the less dominant sexual dimension. Hence, if an individual has a high heteroerotic motivation and low homoerotic motivation, activation of the latter dimension is more likely to occur when a person has high openness to experience. If homoerotic motivation is higher, greater openness to experience is more likely to activate the heterorotic dimension, than for someone with low openness to experience. Activation of the less dominant dimension by some trigger is also more likely to result in exploratory sexual behavior in a person very open to experience, and the experience will further activate that dimension.

Dimension activation and deactivation then plays a very critical role in sexuality—It is not just the presence of masculine, feminine, homoerotic, and heteroerotic dimensions, but whether or not, and to what extent, they become activated or deactivated by external influences. Once activated by modeling and other influences, a person's natural level of the given behavior is expressed. External reinforcement often increases the frequency and intensity of the behavior, thereby shifting the natural range to a higher level. Adverse environmental influences, such as traumatic sexual abuse, can deactivate a dimension and/or reduce the level of motivation. The question arises as to whether or not internal psychological influences also play a role in dimension activation and deactivation? The answer is yes, and the most powerful influence of this type appears to be erotic fantasy, as we will see in the next chapter.

EROTIC FANTASY

Intelligence is a central feature of our evolution. Even at rest the brain consumes about a fifth of the energy we have, making it a very resource intensive adaptation. As a species we have been around about 200,000 years, living in hunting-gathering groups for about 95% of this time, until agriculture developed approximately 10,000 years ago. Hence, the hunting-gathering form of social organization is crucial in understanding our nature, including intelligence. In groups of around 20-100 individuals we moved about in search of game to hunt and quality vegetable items to gather. Lacking the lethal body weaponry of animals like tigers, we relied on group living. Life in these groups was complex, in contrast to the common notion of a simple way of life. Reciprocity was a key feature, due to two main aspects of this way of life, the first being that resources could not be hoarded given how there was no refrigeration, and everything had to be carried when the group moved on. With a shift to agriculture, and even more so an industrial form of social organization, the capacity to hoard items greatly increased. In industrial society individual hoarding of resources is even rewarded and encouraged, with no requirement or expectation to share.

It is highly likely that hoarding as a form of mental illness, well depicted in reality television shows, is based on a distorted and extreme motivation to accumulate resources, in combination with the viability of doing so. That the items hoarded are perceived as valuable is evident by the emotional connection the hoarder feels to the given item. While others see these items as junk for the most part, the hoarder values them. Beyond these examples of extreme hoarding, there is a widespread tendency to monopolize resources, and we now have a situation where about 1% of the population is monopolizing 99% of the wealth. It is not the case that only these individuals seek valuable resources; they are just much better at it than the other 99%, as I cover in At The Tipping Point: How To Save Us From Self-Destruction.

The alternative to hoarding—sharing—was the only viable option, and one that provided a major advantage, and the second aspect of a hunting-gathering way of life that favored reciprocity. What happens if your hunt goes well and that of another person fails? If you share your catch, then that person is indebted to you and will be expected to share when their hunt goes well, and your hunt fails. Keeping track of debts and entitlements is a key feature of hunting-gathering groups, and has structured our social cognition such that we expect fairness. For example, the belief that the world is a fair place, when evidence shows that it is not fair at all, at least within our modern industrial form of social organization. Keeping track of debts and entitlements within hunting-gathering groups required intelligence.

You might say, "Well so what if you don't remember to reciprocate since you always gain by not giving back?" Failure to reciprocate resulted in ostracism by members of the group, the mild version consisting of being excluded from receiving important resources, and the severe version being ejection from the group. Recall that these hunting-gathering groups consisted of about 20-100 individuals interacting with each other daily. It was not like our current industrial society where people frequently interact with strangers, allowing individuals to often get away with not reciprocating. The last thing a person in a hunting-gathering group would want is to be pegged as someone who does not honor debts. Intelligence enabled our ancestors to keep track of whom we owed and who owed us, the latter also very important, as you do not want to lose out. In some hunting-gathering groups debts and entitlements even extended beyond a person's life, with the relatives expected to honor debts and receive entitlements. For example, research by Glantz and Pearce demonstrate that amongst the modern day hunting-gathering Kung Bushmen of the Kalahari, exchange relationships can last a lifetime and beyond, being passed onto a person's offspring. All of this tracking had to be done mentally, as there was no paper and written records. It might well be the case that our hunting-gathering ancestors had better memories than we do, given how memory is currently being outsourced to electronic devices and the Internet.

Additional aspects of a hunting-gathering way of life favored the evolution of intelligence, one being our old friend or enemy, depending on your perspective—Politics. While reciprocity was a key feature of the hunting-gathering way of life, so were hierarchies and status. In what might be described as the "Power of the Hierarchy," we naturally organize ourselves in stratified levels, and view the social landscape in this fashion. The tendency to organize into hierarchies manifests in diverse groupings including, preschool children, early and middle adolescents at summer camp, inmates of penitentiaries, and psychotherapy groups. Put two or more people together and a hierarchy naturally seems to emerge. A key reason for this peculiarity is how our ancestors managed threats. Much like baboon troops, we roamed about typically in areas devoid of trees offering shelter. When a predator attacks, the baboon troop quickly organizes according to the hierarchy, with the dominant male/s, females, and juveniles in the center, and the less dominate males guarding the periphery. This hierarchical structure has proven to be very effective in managing attacks. Imagine a modern day battle scenario where the soldiers respond to an attack in their own individual way, compared to one where a coordinate defense is mounted guided by superiors. Who will fair better? If you chose the former do not consider a career in the military. Navigating political hierarchies involves alliance formation, recruiting support from other members of the group, and responding to status ranking. Intelligence enhances these capacities, thereby improving a person's success within the hierarchy. Positions of dominance were rewarded by preferential access to key resources such as better cuts of meat, more mates, or better quality mates.

Hunting—the predator part of our nature—also fostered intelligence. As a general rule, predators are smarter than prey. Wolves are more intelligent than caribou, raptors more intelligence than the birds they prey on, other birds are more intelligent than the insects they eat. A prey animal just has to try and escape, but a predator has to plan attacks and strategize necessitating intelligence. Lacking the body weaponry of many or most animals we had to do a lot of planning, coordinating, and strategizing to be successful hunters. Our intelligence has transformed us into the ultimate predator, despite limitations in regards to body weaponry. Other animals have evolved intelligence, but revealing a species centric cognitive distortion, we often assume that we are the only one. A litmus test of intelligence is the "mirror test," necessitating that an individual recognizes itself in a mirror. Two-year old children can do this, as can certain animals such as dolphins, great apes, elephants, and some birds such as magpies. Only a limited number of animals have been tested, and so the list will grow. Humans stand out beyond other animals, though, due to our much greater conceptual capacity. The ability of the smartest chimpanzees or gorillas only compares to that of a 3-4 year old child, and no one would say that a young child is all that skilled in terms of conceptual reasoning, compared to a healthy adult. Abstract thinking advances through childhood and the teenage years.

Human intelligence is crucial in understanding human sexuality and sexual orientation, because of a fundamental feature derived from intelligence—The amplification of mental events. Take emotions for example. Certain emotions tend to be primary meaning present in all people—Fear, sadness, anger, disgust, shame, happiness, interest, and surprise, although some researchers debate shame and interest. The universality of these emotions was established by examining societies having no or very little contact with outsiders. Focusing on an isolated New Guinea society, Ekman & Friesen in 1971 gave adults and children three photographs at once, each containing facial expressions of happiness, sadness, anger, disgust, surprise, and fear, and told them a story that involved one emotion. Subjects were able to match stories to facial expressions for the six emotions beyond that predicted by chance. The researchers went one step further having nine New Guineans show how their face would appear if they were the person in the story. The unedited videotapes were shown to college students in the United States. Except for the poses of fear and surprise that the New Guineans had difficulty making faces of, the students accurately recognized the displayed emotion. Supporting the work of Ekman and Friesen, Boucher and Carlson studied Malaysian aboriginals, and found that the same six emotions were recognized in facial expressions with an above average frequency.

A fundamental aspect of emotional information processing is cognitive activating appraisals—Conscious

146

and unconscious thoughts giving rise to our primary emotions. There is a so-called "deep structure" to the cognitive activating appraisals linked to each emotion, constituting a core theme. These deep structures are universal as evidenced by research conducted by Boucher and Carlson in 1980, demonstrating that members of one culture can accurately identify primary emotions from antecedent conditions provided by members of a completely different culture. The deep structures to our primary emotions consist of:

Fear: Threat or danger.
Sadness: Loss.
Happiness: Gain.
Anger: Violation or damage.
Disgust: Contamination of a physical or moral nature.
Shame: The commission of a social transgression.
Interest: The presence of something offering the potential for reward.
Surprise: The sudden appearance of the unexpected, with either positive or negative implications.

Many mammals and primates also demonstrate these primary emotions with the same deep structures applying. Take man's best friend for example. Dogs show interest when a bone is presented, and appear happy to see us when we come home. If there is a threat fear arises, and if attacked anger (expressed as aggression) occurs. When a dog loses its owner sadness seems to ensue. In conducting theoretical work it is important to ask the right question, as unique questions give rise to novel solutions. A crucial question I asked myself, is what would happen when our much greater level of intelligence is superimposed on primary emotions already present? The answer I came up with is that our emotions became amplified, based on intelligence making the underlying cognitive activating appraisals more intensive, extensive, and adding a temporal dimension (Psychological defense mechanisms: A new perspective). So for example, you lose your job and feel sadness based on the loss. Thoughts about all the specific losses like missing your co-workers and nice office intensify the loss. Thinking about circumstances beyond the actual loss extends its impact, as with the thought, "If I lost this job then maybe I don't have what it takes to keep any job." Also highly significant is how intelligence enables us to replay events over time reactivating the relevant emotions. For instance, going over the loss of your job and losses linked to it, keeps reactivating feelings of sadness. People often go over losses, violations, and threats for days, weeks, months, and even years. Many mammals probably just experience the event in the moment and do not replay it in their mind, limiting the impact to the present. More intelligent creatures such as higher primates, dolphins, and elephants seem to experience emotions over time, suggesting that this temporal dimension applies somewhat to them.

The term I coined for the process of intelligence amplifying emotions by making the cognitive activating appraisals more intensive, extensive, and adding a temporal dimension is the "Amplification Effect." It has been said that we are the most emotional of all creatures, and I believe that the amplification effect accounts for this occurrence. The amplification effect also applies to sexuality, the mind being considered by many to be our major sex organ. The amplification of sexuality is evident in our sexual fantasies. Very comprehensive research by Harold Leitenberg and Kris Henning (Sexual fantasy), demonstrates how prevalent sexual fantasies are. The studies they reviewed occurred before the explosion of sexuality on the Internet that could be said to drive sexual fantasies. For example, if men fantasize about sex with a few women at one time, is it because they see it on a website or multiple websites? Or is it a more natural fantasy? Leitenburg and Henning examined studies exploring different themes, such as the number of men and women who report having sexual fantasies during masturbation. Based on the 13 studies reviewed the range for men was 50% to 100%, with the mean 85.9%. For women the range was 31% to 100%, with a mean of 68.8%. Clearly, most men and women engage in sexual fantasy during masturbation. What about during intercourse? Of 7 studies reporting on men the range was 47% to 92%, with an average of 76%. The range for the 12 studies assessing women's fantasies during intercourse was 34% to 94%, with an average of 70%. These results for sexual fantasy during intercourse are very revealing, because they demonstrate that even during the most classic of sexual acts our brains are hard at work generating fantasy.

If we so readily engage in sexual fantasy during masturbation and intercourse, then it follows that we are likely to be fantasizing when there is no sexual outlet. The 3 studies reviewed by Leitenberg and Henning, assessing this in men, gave a range of 82% to 100%, with an average of 93%. The 5 studies assessing it in females provided a range of 77% to 100%, with a mean of 84.8%. Based on a study by Cameron (Note on time spent thinking about sex), many people think of a sexual fantasy within a given 5-minute period; 52% of men and 39% of women in the 14-25 year age range, and 26% of men and 14% of women in the 26-55 year age range. Evidently, a significant portion of our thinking is devoted to sexual fantasy during masturbation, intercourse, and when not engaged in a sexual act. It truly is a pronounced amplification effect based on the evolution of human intelligence. Some readers might be wondering if animals also engage in sexual fantasy? Understandably, that is a very difficult issue to assess, but based on the limited conceptual ability of even the most intelligent of animals, it appears likely that it is absent or at most highly limited.

The meaning or reason for our intensive and extensive sexual fantasy can and has been debated. Sigmund Freud believed that sexual fantasy represents a compensation for inadequate sexuality. Freud wrote, "A happy person never phantisizes, only an unsatisfied one." Individuals with sexual fantasies are sexually repressed, and the fantasy expresses their sex drive. His patient population consisted primarily of young middle-class Jewish Viennese women, who were highly sexually repressed within their conservative family environment, as suggested by Edward Shorter in A History Of Psychiatry (as also mentioned the Psychological Theories chapter). Shorter argues that this highly select sexually repressed patient sample was instrumental in the sexual nature of his theories. In contrast to Freud's perspective, evidence overwhelmingly indicates that sexual fantasy is a healthy and normal component of sexuality. Those who have frequent sexual fantasies are healthier sexually with, "drive induction" as opposed to "drive reduction." Leitenburg and Henning in their review paper, indicate that women and men who experience orgasm more frequently during intercourse and masturbation have more, and not less, sexual fantasy.

Greater ability to be sexually aroused also aligns with more sexual fantasy, and those who have robust sexual fantasies often have more varied and fulfilling sexual lives. For example, Lentz and Zeiss (Fantasy and sexual arousal in college women: An empirical investigation) found that women with more erotic fantasies during masturbation, experience more frequent orgasms during intercourse. Kinsey and colleagues in 1953 (Sexual Behavior In The Human Female) even found that some women achieve orgasm just by fantasizing! Crepault and Coulture (Men's erotic fantasies) found that men having more frequent sexual fantasies during intercourse tend to be more sexually active generally, with more erotic fantasies outside of sexual activity, better capacity to control the timing of ejaculation, a more active role in sex, and other indicators of heightened sexuality, such as experimentation with homoerotic behavior.

Appreciating that sexual fantasy relates to enhanced sexuality and performance, it is understandable that it is applied to treat sexual problems. A basic technique in sex therapy is to encourage the client to engage in sexual fantasies during masturbation and intercourse, and also when not engaging in sexual activity. Zeiss and colleagues (Orgasm during intercourse: A treatment strategy for women) found that women instructed to engage in fantasy during solitary masturbation, were more likely to experience orgasm during sex. Sexual fantasy then expresses and motivates healthy sexuality, and does not serve as a compensation for impaired sexuality.

A major impediment to healthy sexuality is guilt, because it often blocks sexual fantasy. We live in a very guilt oriented world, based on Christian-Muslim-Jewish values. People often think of these religions as being highly distinct, but they are all cut from the same cloth, and one that is not very open to sexual expression. A likely reason why there has been so much friction and fighting between followers of these religions since their inception, is how similar they are, the conflict emphasizing differences that distinguish them. In addition, sexual

151

frustration arising from the sexually repressive nature of these religions is likely transformed into anger and aggression, resulting in heightened conflict. If anyone doubts how sexually repressive these religions are, a quick look at history will cast aside any doubts. Ancient Greek and Roman societies were much more open to diverse sexual expressions, including homoerotic behavior. Their artwork, sculptures, architecture, and writings provide ample evidence of this openness. Even the ancient Egyptians were more open to sexuality allowing its expression in temple drawings. Early Christians (Coptics) frequently defaced temples, removing sexual imagery.

Moving ahead to more recent times, guilt impedes sexual fantasy and consequently healthy sexuality. Sexual satisfaction tends to be related to the frequency of sexual fantasy—The more fantasy the more satisfaction. For example, Cado and Leitenberg (Guilt reactions to sexual fantasies during intercourse), found less sexual fantasy, more sexual problems, less sexual satisfaction in general, and more discontentment with their current or most recent partner, in people who felt the most guilt about having sexual fantasies during intercourse. Other studies have not found a relationship between fantasy and sexual satisfaction, but sexual satisfaction might not be an ideal measure of the importance of fantasy; actual sexual behavior and its relationship to sexual fantasy is probably a better indicator. In this regard it appears that sexual fantasy is related to a more active sex life—As indicated by Leitenburg and Henning in their review article, studies have revealed that sexual fantasy is related to a higher frequency of masturbation and intercourse, more lifetime partners, and greater self-rated sex drive.

Sexual fantasies appear to arise at a young age, corresponding approximately with the onset of puberty.

Leitenburg and Henning indicate that studies reveal the age of onset at around 11-13 years of age. Gold and Gold (Gender differences in first sexual fantasies), examining heterosexuals found that the mean age of the first sexual fantasy recalled was 11.5 years for males, and 12.9 years for females. Examining the early sexual fantasies of gay men Lehne (Gay male fantasies and realities), found that the mean age of their first gay fantasy, as recalled by these men, was 12.2 years. 12% reported fantasies before 10 years of age, and 83% prior to 13 years of age. Hence, research clearly indicates that sexual fantasies emerge around the time of puberty for men and women, of both a heterosexual and homosexual orientation.

Content of erotic fantasies is worth exploring. Given the power of thought a highly diverse range of fantasies is to be expected, and research supports this. Reviewing a large number of studies reporting on the content of sexual fantasy, Leitenburg and Henning suggest that the three most common types for both sexes are, reliving an exciting sexual experience, imagining sex with one's current partner, and imagining sex with another partner. Differences between men and women have been found, a theme being that women tend to be more aroused by fantasies of emotional closeness and a narrative of being valued in some way, whereas men's fantasies contain more visual imagery and explicit anatomical detail. Romance novels such as Harlequin account for something in the order of 40% of paperback sales, and are almost exclusively purchased by women. In contrast, men account for almost all the sales of pornographic magazines and online sites. The magazine, Playgirl designed for women, sells mostly to gay men. An evolutionary explanation appears to have merit—During evolution men were the pursuers and had to look for signs of receptivity in females, hence the visual and explicit detail focus.

Women being limited in terms of the number of children they can have and successfully rear (reproductive potential), instead seek signs of quality in males, and also the willingness and capacity of a mate to provide resources. The fantasy of an appealing man being close to them and attentive aligns with the reproductive potential motivation.

A very interesting, consistent, and puzzling aspect of sexual fantasy in women that has emerged is submission or so-called "rape" fantasies. Several different studies have shown that women are more likely than men to fantasize, even during intercourse, about being forced to submit. These fantasies are actually in the top favorite sexual fantasies of women, and emerge in research conducted across several decades indicating a persistent occurrence. Joseph Critelli and Jenny Bivona in Women's erotic rape fantasies: An evaluation of theory and research, examined this fascinating occurrence. Many different theories and associated events have been proposed to account for it. Some believe that women with these fantasies are more subservient in a traditional sense, but research shows that they are just as likely to be feminists. It has been suggested that they have experienced rape and are replaying it, but women with submission fantasies are actually less likely to have been raped. Openness to experience appears to play a role, in that these fantasies are more common in women who have experienced a greater variety of sex acts, had more sexual partners, and fantasize more about sex in general, as found in a study by Pelletier and Herold (The relationship of age, sex guilt, and sexual experience with female sexual fantasies).

The term "submission" fantasy is more appropriate than "rape" fantasy, because during a rape an individual has no control, making it a universally traumatic

154

experience. When women fantasize about being taken sexually they control the fantasy, typically generating a theme of a powerful man (read a man with resources) desiring them, and valuing them enough to make the effort to dominate them. This recurrent theme aligns with the evolutionary explanation of women focusing on men with resources, who will assist them in rearing offspring. Furthermore, given that women have control over their submission fantasy, they keep the level of aggression within comfortable limits. They are also able to see themselves as attractive and desirable, thereby enhancing self-esteem, given that the male desires them over others.

So far the presentation has largely focused on heteroerotic activity, but what about homoerotic fantasy. Although less research has examined this matter, based on the review by Leitenburg and Henning and other data, it appears that there are more similarities than differences, other than for the gender of the imagined partner. So for example, lesbians have submission fantasies as do heterosexual women, but the submission is to a powerful woman instead of a man. Male homosexuals tend to have visual fantasies pertaining to explicit body parts, but the penis or male buttocks is the focus, as opposed to female breasts or pubic region. A large and representative study by Price and colleagues (Comparison of sexual fantasies of homosexuals and heterosexuals) shows how homo and hetero fantasies are similar. The top 5 sexual fantasies for homosexual men in their sample were, unspecified sexual activity with another man, performing oral sex, having a partner perform oral sex, participating in anal sex, and sex with a new partner. The top 5 sexual fantasies for heterosexual men in their sample were, having their partner perform oral sex, performing oral sex, anticipating sexual activity with the current partner, having sex with more than one partner at the same time, and being with a new partner. The top 5 sexual fantasies for lesbians were, unspecified sexual activity with another partner, having their partner perform oral sex, performing oral sex, anticipating sexual activity with their partner, and being held and touched. The top 5 for the heterosexual women consisted of, anticipating sexual activity with their current partner, having the partner perform oral sex, being irresistible to the opposite sex, having sex with more than one person at a time, and being held and touched. Research shows that homosexuals, like heterosexuals, engage in frequent sexual fantasy with strong similarities to heterosexual fantasy consistent with gender, although reversing the gender of the desired partners.

Sexual fantasies appear to amplify all aspects of sexuality, including preferences for certain types of sex. You perform oral sex on a partner or partners and really enjoy the experience, meaning that it is very rewarding. Due to how rewarding it has been you will tend to repeat it, a process referred to as operant conditioning—You performed an operation (act) and the response was so positive you are motivated to repeat it. Fantasizing about the act when not sexually active, during masturbation, and when engaging in actual sex, amplifies your desire and motivation for performing the act. A different form of conditioning known as classical conditioning can transform nonsexual objects into sexual ones, amplifying sex beyond inherently sexual stimuli. For example, a teenage boy notices an attractive woman wearing a skirt, so short that her public region is somewhat exposed when she sits down. Since the pubic region is tightly linked to sex it represents an unconditioned stimulus, meaning that it naturally elicits a sexual response, labeled an unconditioned response. The short skirt that the woman is wearing is not a natural sexual object. The linkage of the short skirt to the unconditioned stimulus of her partially exposed pubic region, transforms it into a conditioned stimulus, producing a conditioned response of sexual arousal. However, unless the pairing is repeated the linkage fades, and the short skirt itself will fail to elicit a sexual arousal response. While it is possible that the teenage boy might see enough instances of short skirts and partially exposed pubic regions to maintain the pairing, often this does not occur. What maintains the linkage is erotic fantasy. The teenager fantasizes about the partially exposed pubic region and short skirt, imagining various scenarios involving the combination, and masturbates in response to these images. He even imagines it when not masturbating and starts to become aroused. The erotic fantasy maintains and amplifies the classical conditioning.

Conditioning and its amplification via erotic fantasy plays a major role in paraphilic disorders—Fetishism, frotteurism, transvestic fetishism, exhibitionism, and sadomasochism. Fetishism is an extreme version of the short skirt example provided above, and occurs when the strength of the sexual arousal to a nonsexual object is so intense that it causes distress or interferes with functioning. For example, the teenage boy is only aroused by short skirts and is not interested in sexual contact, short skirts now eliciting much more of a sexual response than the pubic region they were initially linked to. Performing sexually with women might not be possible causing distress for the individual. While the cause of paraphilic disorders is not clear at this time, all seem to involve an aberrant conditioning process and erotic fantasy, at least to some extent. For example, a man's pelvic region accidently bumps against a woman's buttocks on a subway and he experiences arousal. Afterwards, on another crowded train he sees a woman beside him, and starts fantasizing about his pelvic region brushing against her buttocks. He then acts on the fantasy and experiences arousal. Operant conditioning has occurred, and as he fantasizes about the behavior his sexual arousal in response to this type of contact is amplified. Further repetitions of the actual behavior and erotic fantasy produce the paraphilia of so-called frotteurism.

Transvestic fetishism occurs when dressing in clothes of the opposite sex produces sexual arousal. This is in marked contrast to gender identity issues, occurring when a person feels as if they are other than their biological sex, and dresses in a fashion that is appropriate for the other gender. There is no sexual arousal involved in this scenario, dress aligning with who they feel they really are in terms of gender. In my clinical experience, males with transvestic fetishism (I cannot recall seeing a female with the condition) all have a very robust sexual drive. Typically, they try on their partner's clothes when sexually aroused, become more aroused by the act and subsequent fantasy about it, and then masturbate in response to the erotic fantasy. Both operant and classical conditioning play a role. Operant in that the person engages in an action that is rewarded with enhanced sexual arousal. Classical based on the inherently nonsexual clothing item being transformed into a conditioned stimulus, producing the conditioned response of sexual arousal. The person then fantasizes about dressing in female clothing, amplifying the arousal and enhancing the conditioning process.

The other two forms of paraphilic disorders—exhibitionism and sadomasochism—might be less influenced by conditioning, but still can involve operant and classical conditioning, and certainly erotic fantasy. Exhibitionists frequently generate cognitive distortions, such as believing that the viewer will respond sexually. This distorted perspective regarding the viewer's response can reinforce the act of exposing oneself (operant conditioning). Being nude is not necessarily sexual, but the act of exposing body parts can transform nudity into a conditioned stimulus producing a sexualized response. As with the other paraphilias erotic fantasy about exposing oneself amplifies the arousal. Additional factors, such as poor impulse control appear to play a role in exhibitionism.

Sadomasochism is a complex entity, and probably is for the most part not a disorder. For example, Richters and colleagues (Demographic and psychosocial features of participants in bondage and discipline, "sadomasochism" or dominance and submission (BDSM): Data from a national survey) found that it is a sexual interest, and not pathology related to past abuse or sexual problems. Conditioning amplified by erotic fantasy almost certainly plays a key role. For example, a female's partner lightly spanks her on the buttocks when she is sexually aroused, and she becomes more aroused by engaging in a submission fantasy. The spanking action and submission to it has produced a pleasurable sexual response amplified by fantasy, resulting in operant conditioning. In addition, spanking becomes a conditioned stimulus. When it repeats she engages in further submission fantasies of her own design amplifying the arousal, thereby strengthening the operant and classical conditioning process. In the rare instances that a person engages in very dangerous high-risk behaviors such as suffocation, then other factors, such as childhood abuse and personality disorders, are likely at work, transforming a sexual interest into pathology.

EROTIC FANTASY & SEXUAL ORIENTATION:

Considering the powerful role that erotic fantasy plays in all aspects of sexuality, it is understandable that it be put forward as a cause or instrumental factor in sexual orientation. Daryl Bem (Exotic becomes erotic: A developmental theory of sexual orientation) proposes that biology plays an indirect role in sexual orientation, by influencing childhood temperaments that guide a child's preferences for sex-typical or sex-atypical activities and peers. Due to "atypical" preferences the child feels different from other or same-sex peers, the exotic part. The heightened physiological (autonomic) arousal based on feeling different than same-sex individuals, later becomes eroticized to sexual arousal for that same class of peers, a process he refers to as "sexual imprinting."

Despite it being a very creative theory and incorporating erotic fantasy, there are some major problems with it. For one, many "gay" individuals do not always have preferences different than same-sex peers. The notion that gay men are effeminate and lesbians are masculine is a stereotype that is not born out by research data, or at best only partially, as we have seen. Many gay men have very gender typical preferences, as do lesbian women. The gender atypical ones (effeminate gay men and masculine lesbians) have a much more difficult time hiding their orientation, and hence are more likely to be "out." This occurrence alters our perception of what homosexual men and women are like. One gay male engineer in my practice engaged in traditionally "masculine" pursuits, such as working on electronic circuits as a child and teenager. There was nothing "atypical" about his gender preferences other than a strong attraction for same-sex peers. I have seen many other instances of homosexuality and gender typical behavior, as well as heterosexuality and gender atypical behavior, such as one man with very robust heteroerotic urges, including for threesomes with two women, who has always loved expressive dance. He meets several of his partners at dance events.

The second problem with Bem's theory is that it really only makes sense within a dichotomized sexual orientation world—The theory is based on the notion that people are homosexual, heterosexual, or bisexual (as odd as the latter is to process in a dichotomized world). As we have seen, though, there are separate homoerotic and heteroerotic dimensions in each of us, providing the capacity for both forms of behavior. This occurrence eliminates the need to explain dichotomous sexual orientations. A third problem with the theory is that there is no solid evidence that physiological arousal derived from "atypical" preferences, can transform into an erotic state, or in other words exotic lead to erotic. Possibly through some conditioning process this might be feasible, but there is no evidence that sexual orientation is a conditioned response, and indeed homoerotic and heteroerotic behavior manifest quite naturally in the absence of operant and classical conditioning.

Erotic fantasy actually plays a much more profound role in sexual orientation than what a theory such as Bem's suggests—Erotic fantasy adds an entire layer of sexuality beyond actual behavior! When we consider sexuality in animals we focus on sexual acts, in part because that is all that is visible, but also due to how animals probably do not engage in erotic fantasy. Perhaps the most intelligent animals, such as dolphins and great apes, might have some fantasy, but overall the role of erotic fantasy in animals is likely negligible. In contrast, for humans erotic fantasy is at least as important to sexuality as actual behavior, meaning that it adds another level or layer to sexual orientation. Anyone doubting the value of erotic fantasy to human sexual orientation must consider this question—If a person engages in erotic fantasy that is exclusively focused on same-sex individuals, but only partakes in sex with other-sex individuals, what sexual orientation do they best fit into?

Given the private nature of erotic fantasy there is no censorship or negative influence, unless derived from a person's own guilt, hence it tends to be a more accurate indicator of a person's level of homoerotic and heteroerotic motivation. Actual behavior is a much different story with a multitude of factors impacting on it. Discrimination against homosexuals is very common today, even in more civilized parts of the world, and to escape persecution many people refrain from acting on their homoerotic desires. A woman or man might want a child and marry to achieve this goal, suppressing homoerotic urges to maintain the marriage. Countless other influences on homoerotic and heteroerotic expressions occur, ensuring that actual behavioral manifestations are a less reliable indicator of a person's relative levels of homoerotic and heteroerotic motivation than is erotic fantasy. One such influence is guilt induced by the larger society based on a homosexual orientation being viewed as less desirable, or in other words having a lower social value associated with it. Due to the prevailing social values some people feel guilty for even homoerotic fantasies, but the intensity of guilt is usually far greater for actual acts. So long as a desire stays as a thought it tends to be okay, but when transformed into an action the reaction is much more intense. For example, you might fantasize about killing a particularly nasty boss, with many coworkers empathizing with you, but if you actually do it few would be supportive. The guilt many experience in response to acting in accordance with their homoerotic desires, often blocks those urges from being expressed in actual behavior.

Kinsey believed that sexual orientation should be defined primarily in terms of the type, extent, and frequency of a person's erotic fantasies. Assessing these erotic fantasies in many people he proposed the, at that time, revolutionary notion of sexual orientation being on a continuum and not dichotomous. Storms' two-dimensional model with homoerotic and heteroerotic dimensions is also based on erotic fantasy. The models proposed by Kinsey and Storms both predict that those having a homosexual orientation have stronger same-sex erotic fantasies, and those with a heterosexual orientation have more powerful other-sex erotic fantasies. The models also predict that bisexuals have more same-sex erotic fantasies than heterosexuals and more other-sex erotic fantasies than homosexuals.

Kinsey and Storms models diverge in their predictions of the relative strength of homoerotic fantasies between bisexuals and homosexuals, and strength of heteroerotic fantasies between bisexuals and heterosexuals—Based on the structure of Kinsey's single dimension it predicts that bisexuals have weaker homoerotic fantasies than homosexuals and weaker heteroerotic fantasies than heterosexuals, whereas Storms' model suggests that bisexuals can have homoerotic fantasy equal or even greater to those of homosexuals, as well as heteroerotic fantasies as strong or stronger than heterosexuals. The latter prediction is born out, providing solid proof that human sexuality is two-dimensional in nature. In addition, Kinsey's model must place asexuals off the single dimension, or if on the scale equivalent in erotic fantasy to bisexuals, a truly absurd scenario. Storms' two-dimensional model accurately places asexuals as having very low homoerotic and heteroerotic fantasies. The scales Kinsey and Storms used both assess homoerotic and heteroerotic fantasy, as do many other scales that have been devised to evaluate sexual orientation. Kinsey's scale is called the Heterosexual-Homosexual Rating Scale. Ratings of 1-5, meaning not exclusively homosexual or heterosexual are based on desires (fantasy) for sexual activity with either sex. For a 0 rating (exclusive heterosexuality) or 6 (exclusive homosexuality), a person has no experience or desire for the same-sex (0) or other-sex (6). Storms' scale is named the Erotic Response and Orientation Scale (EROS), strictly assessing erotic fantasy. These scales and the models of Kinsey and Storms highlight the powerful role that erotic fantasy plays in human sexual orientation.

Erotic fantasy also plays a secondary, but still very powerful, role in sexuality—Activation of the homoerotic and heteroerotic dimensions. When a person engages in a homoerotic fantasy that dimension is activated, as is the heteroerotic dimension with heteroerotic fantasy. An individual's level of motivation for the given behavior will then emerge, often leading to sexual acts and/or further fantasy. The power of erotic fantasy to activate sexual orientation dimensions is likely instrumental in how motivation can increase over time, consistent with the notion of sexuality being a fluid and dynamic process capable of varying throughout the life cycle. For example, if a person has a pleasing homoerotic relationship during adolescence, erotic fantasy over time about this experience will continuously activate the homoerotic dimension. This activation will increase the likelihood of additional homoerotic experiences, and the resulting erotic fantasy will further intensify homoerotic motivation. Erotic fantasy can then reinforce and hence increase activation of homoerotic and heteroerotic

164

dimensions, and even keep a dimension activated when it cannot be expressed. For example, a woman with a higher heteroerotic motivation identifies with being straight, but fantasizes about a homoerotic relationship consistent with significant homoerotic motivation. The erotic fantasy keeps the dimension activated despite an absence of homoerotic encounters.

Erotic fantasy and its influence on homoerotic and heteroerotic dimension activation, also helps account for the impact of sexual abuse on subsequent sexual behavior. When a person is sexually abused even in childhood some pleasure can be experienced, perhaps just from the attention being paid to the individual. Those who sexually abuse children or adolescents frequently are quite attentive to the immediate needs of those they abuse, and are violent only in a minority of instances, as discussed previously in the Homoerotic & Heteroerotic Dimension Activation chapter. Erotic fantasy, facilitated by the pleasure and attention component, keeps the relevant sexual orientation dimension (homoerotic if same-sex and heteroerotic if other-sex) activated by amplifying sexual arousal for the incident. On the other hand, if the abuse was violent, frightening, or damaging, erotic fantasy will often be blocked, thereby deactivating the relevant sexual orientation dimension and reducing or eliminating sexual interest. The ability of erotic fantasy (or its absence) to activate or deactivate sexual orientation dimensions, aligns with the capacity of cognitive activity to augment or inhibit sexual response cycles, as reported by Walen and Roth. The interaction between erotic fantasy and the activation of our homoerotic and heteroerotic dimensions, can then account for some of the more puzzling aspects of human sexuality.

The brain is undoubtedly our most powerful sex organ and without it human sexuality would be very different. Indeed, it is almost impossible to imagine human sexuality divorced from our imagination (excuse the pun). Erotic fantasy provides us with a depth and extent of sexuality experienced by no other animal. First and foremost, erotic fantasy constitutes a layer of sexual orientation above and beyond actual behavior. If that was not enough, erotic fantasy is actually a more representative component of our sexual orientation than physical behavior, highlighting the power of the human mind. The role of erotic fantasy in the activation/deactivation of our homoerotic and heteroerotic dimensions provides a secondary, but still very important, way that erotic fantasy influences sexual orientation.

SOCIAL CONSTRUCTION

Much of what we are familiar with is constructed. Take your house or apartment building, place of employment, car, and all the other items that you rely on. While readers will readily acknowledge that this is so, the notion of non-physical entities being constructed is less straightforward, and even odd. However, if we consider many social conventions, such as holiday celebrations, it is evident that they must have been created. The Happy Birthday song was written, family members and friends gather to celebrate a person's special day, it had to become established that a birthday is an event to celebrate, a cake with candles is provided, the person blows out the candles following the song, makes a wish, and then opens presents. When you consider it the whole scenario is vey much designed and assembled, despite the absence of a permanent physical structure such as a house.

In considering the birthday example, the notion that things are inherent and not influenced by us seems unlikely. Why would a birthday celebration be absolute and set? No animal species celebrates birthdays, and throughout most of our evolution people were unlikely to have tracked their age nor had the means to, cake and candles did not exist, and the birthday song was not yet written. The concept that things are inherent and outside our control is known as essentialism. Things simply are, and we do not influence them with our actions or thoughts. In 1966 Peter Berger and Thomas Luckman challenged this view in their book, The Social Construction Of Reality. They argued that all knowledge, even everyday commonsense notions, arise from and are maintained by social interactions. People enter into these interactions aware that their perceptions of reality are related. The shared awareness and interactions based upon them reinforce the understanding. Over time if the pattern is repeated frequently and by enough people, it becomes established as objective reality, and hence has been socially constructed. Take our example of the traditional birthday celebration. The birthday person, and his or her family members and friends, are all aware that the purpose is to recognize another year of life as a positive event. This awareness and the ceremony based upon it, strengthen knowledge that the whole event is a celebration of aging. Its repetition over many years and by enough people, resulted in it becoming a socially constructed part of objective reality. However, this is not to say that it is an immutable event, as some people chose not to have a birthday celebration, and in many cultures other traditions associated with aging occur.

Social construction can generally take two forms—Strong (also known as radical or extreme) and weak (also referred to as mild or contextual). The strong version opposes "brute" facts, maintaining that everything is a creation and lacks an objective reality. In its strictest interpretation there is no actual birthday or anything corresponding to it, we just create the entity. There are problems with the strong interpretation making it quite weak, one being that there is usually a corresponding real entity. For example, with birthdays there is an actual year related to 365 days of the Earth's rotation around the sun. Another problem is that if there is nothing objective or real, then logically researching the entity is without merit. Hence, strong social construction itself should never be researched, and even if so it can never be established to truly exist because it is only a social creation. Social construction is frequently attacked and critiqued on the basis of the strong interpretation. This negative input is understandable in one sense, given how weak and vulnerable to critique the strong version is. Some social construction researchers, such as Sismondo (Some social constructions. Social studies of science), view this as completely unwarranted, because the vast majority of research does not argue for the strong perspective. Most empirical research adopts a relative or contextual perspective maintaining that there is an objective reality, with the study attempting to define how it is expressed or interpreted.

The weak version, being more relative and reasonable, is actually quite strong. It acknowledges that there is a real entity, but that how this is expressed or interpreted is a social construction. Birthdays correspond to something real but how the event is expressed or understood can vary widely, depending upon how it is socially constructed. Disease is a real entity that can be researched, but how we understand it can vary depending upon our interpretation. Heart disease for example might be constructed in a heroic narrative fashion, whereby a person, usually a man, bravely faces the rigors of life but is eventually worn down by it all. Another interpretation, much more negative and blame oriented, is that the person is lazy and did not bother to look after his or her health. Still another is that it is all about having the right genetic material, and if you have bad genes then heart attacks at an earlier age can occur. All of these social constructions represent different expressions or interpretations of the underlying objective heart disease entity.

When it comes to sexuality, a real entity definitely exists in that sexual behavior is alive and well in countless species, many with limited social organization, and sexuality is expressed in people even when isolated. In addition, there is ample biological research data supporting the presence of organic influences on sexual functioning. A key problem with human sexual orientation is that we often take the perspective that it is immutable and essentially essential. I hope that readers note the irony of us taking a perspective that something is completely objective. It is understood that there are real heterosexual and homosexual entities, with the former difficult to understand based on our certainty that the purpose of sex is for reproduction, hence the evolutionary or Darwinian paradox. We are so embedded in this understanding of sexual orientation that is has to be real, right? Well, maybe not.

As we have seen there are homoerotic and heteroerotic dimensions in each of us providing some capacity for both behaviors. A higher level of motivation on the homoerotic dimension aligns with "homosexuality," and the reverse profile with "heterosexuality," whereas a robust level on both dimensions equates with bisexuality. However, "homosexuality" and "heterosexuality" are not real entities in and of themselves, but more descriptions of natural occurrences. Approaching the social construction of sexual orientation from another perspective, Michael Foucault in his 1980 book, The History Of Sexuality, proposed that instead of homosexuality being a real entity it has been created by us! His perspective is that based on the practice of sodomy, homosexuality was transformed from a temporary aberration into a new species. We have created the dichotomous categories of homosexuality and heterosexuality, and now are puzzled by the former. It is similar to saying that the traditional birthday celebration is an immutable objective reality, and then trying to figure out why we have to be so positive about aging.

170

In line with social construction theory there are strong and weak versions of homosexuality. The strong version is that nothing real corresponds to it at all. However, based on the material that has been presented so far regarding animal homoerotic behavior, dimensions of sexual orientation derived from the animal sexuality templates, and adaptive functions of the homoerotic and heteroerotic dimensions, I hope that no reader will be inclined to believe that homosexuality is 100% created. There is indeed an objective reality corresponding to it, in terms of animal homoerotic behavior and the homoerotic dimension present in all of us. Those with a high rating on the homoerotic dimension and much lower rating on the heteroerotic dimension, identify with being homosexual. However, identifying with what might only be a socially constructed entity does not make it real, beyond the reality we create. Indeed, if both homoerotic and heteroerotic dimensions are present in us all, how can anyone be exclusively homosexual lacking any capacity to function heterosexually? Perhaps if there is a zero motivation on the heterosexual dimension, it could be argued that there is absolute homosexuality, but as we have seen this might only be an illusion arising from deactivation or suppression of that dimension, based on traumatic heteroerotic sexual abuse or mental illness. It has been my intention to open you up to the possibility that homosexuality, at least as we understand it, is largely a social construction. Yes, there is a reality that corresponds somewhat to it, but homosexuality is only one of many ways that this more objective reality can be expressed and understood. To gain a greater appreciation for how we have constructed sexual orientation, it is informative to take a look at the ways that sexuality has been conceptualized in different cultures over time.

Humans have been around for approximately 200,000 years, 95% of that time in hunting-gathering groups. Our early ancestors left very little documentation of their way of life including sexuality. We do know, though, that human homoerotic behavior dates well back into prehistory, based upon 17,000-year old Paleolithic cave paintings showing male erections in contact with each other (as mentioned earlier in the book). However, it is really only when we get to more formal civilizations that solid recorded evidence exists. The clearest example is ancient Greek society, with evidence of homoerotic behavior in writings such as the dialogues of Plato, plays, and art. As it turns out, their culture did not have any actual terms or concepts corresponding to our understanding of heterosexuality and homosexuality, and there were various themes related to homoerotic behavior and sexuality. One of the most recurrent themes is beauty, and the acceptability of being drawn to it in either sex. An Athenian general and politician in the 5th century B.C—Alcibiades—was described by Diogenes Laeurtius as, "In his adolescence he drew away the husbands from their wives, and as a young man the wives from their husbands." Life and sexuality was to a large extent a celebration of beauty. A character in Plutarch's Erotikos (Dialogues on love) puts forward, "The noble lover of beauty engages in love wherever he sees excellence and splendid natural endowment without regard for any difference in physiological detail." Although we appreciate beauty in both sexes, we currently do not base our sexual attraction on it, at least irrespective of gender.

An exclusive interest in gender occurred but appears to have been the exception. Alexander the Great was known for only being interested in boys and other men, but it was more common for people to have erotic relationships with both sexes. Much more relevant to ancient Greek society was status, and the related role that should be played in erotic relationships. A full citizen, essentially an adult male who was not a slave, had a high status, and based on this standing was to act in the role of penetrator. Boys, young men, adult men without status, and women were to be penetrated, but the citizen should not be penetrated. Given that all adult free males were citizens homoerotic relationships between them was not acceptable—One person has to get penetrated and neither was allowed to be. Hence, the ideal was a homoerotic relationship between an adult man, often in his 20's or 30's known as erastes, and a boy whose beard had not yet grown, referred to as eromenos or paidika. Relative to our cultural norms this might appear as abuse, but there was honor involving a courtship ritual. The erastes was to show interest beyond sex and provide gifts. The eromenos was not to submit too easily, and select the highest-ranking suitor. At times sex was intercrural, whereby the man placed his penis between the thighs of his young lover, avoiding anal penetration. These relationships were temporary ending when the boy reached adulthood, but given the reciprocal and non-abusive nature often formed the basis of ongoing friendships and alliances. Homoerotic relationships between younger and older males were also practiced in ancient China, Japan, Islamic nations, and the earliest recording in ancient Greece date to 800 BC.

In ancient Greek culture attraction to other men was seen as a sign of masculinity. Their Gods such as Zeus were said to engage in same-sex relationships, as did their heroes in myth and literature, such as Achilles and Hercules. An army regiment of 500 male same-sex lovers, the Sacred Band Of Thebes, was known for their valor in battle. Plato, in the Symposium argues for an army to be comprised of same-sex lovers. Consider in comparison how our modern day militaries, such as that of the United States, largely rejected "gays." Yes, we live in a very different world apparently not due to any objective reality, but based on subjective perspectives and ways of understanding homoerotic relationships.

Moving ahead in time to ancient Roman civilization we see, at least initially, a similar pattern to that of ancient Greece. Relationships between older free men and males not yet men were the norm. Apparently all the emperors other than Claudius took male lovers. The similarity to ancient Greek culture characterized the Republic, but began to change with the Empire influenced by the rise of Christianity. Early Christians or Coptics took a dim view of many forms of sexual expression, actually cutting penises and other symbols of sexuality off temples, as is evident on the Egyptian temples built by the ancient Greeks and Romans. The Christian emperor of ancient Rome, Theodosius I, decreed on August 6, 390 A.D. that passive males were to be burned at the stake. In 558 A.D. Justinian expanded this proscription (the Justinian Code) to include the active partner, warning that such conduct can lead to the destruction of cities through the "wrath of God." Quite a radical shift from the way that homoerotic relationships were conceptualized prior to this time. With the late Romans there was a definite shift to intolerance based largely on the Christian influence, but much regional variation occurred.

Ironically, with the fall of the Roman Empire more tolerance of homoerotic relationships occurred throughout Europe. Even though several Christian theologians denounced sex not leading to procreation, some of the clergy produced pro homoerotic literature, particularly in the eleventh and twelve century. Starting in the thirteenth century, persecution of homoerotic behavior increased, alongside persecution of Jews,

174

Muslims, and others not part of the mainstream. A very interesting aspect of this sexual persecution was that it targeted the behavior of sodomy, because it does not lead to procreation. Hence, male-to-female sodomy was opposed, along with male-to-male. Sodomites were those who engaged in the act of sodomy, as opposed to a sexual orientation designation. The focus was on the actual act of sodomy rather than gender, although certain theologians argued that same-sex sodomy was worse. Some of those who engaged in sodomy were executed by being burned or beheaded, but often if a person repented and vowed never to do it again, they were no longer considered a sodomite and spared execution. Over the next several centuries, anti-sodomy laws were enforced sporadically. In the 1730's the Dutch launched a major campaign, even using torture to extract confessions. Up to 100 men and boys were executed and denied burial.

During the Renaissance same-sex relationships, even those involving sodomy became more open, particularly in Florence and Venice. Meanwhile, under the aegis of the Officers of the Night Court, a significant percentage of the population was being prosecuted, fined, and imprisoned for such behavior. During the nineteenth century legal penalties for sodomy declined markedly. The Napoleonic Code decriminalized sodomy, and with Napoleon's conquests the Code spread. Secular rather than religious perspectives came to dominate, diluting the focus on sodomy and non-procreative actions. At the very least, sodomy was removed from the list of capital crimes, and no one was executed. It is amazing relative to our focus on sexual orientation, how Europe for centuries was concentrating on the act of sodomy regardless of same-sex or other-sex relationships.

Perhaps homoerotic relationships only occurred in the European area, given a fairly common cultural background heavily influenced by ancient Greek and Roman civilizations. Countering this possibility, the evidence overwhelmingly indicates that homoerotic relationships were the norm and not the exception. For example, in Japan such relationships between men, known as shudo or nanshoku, were documented over a thousand years ago. In fact, they were an essential part of the Buddhist monastic life and the samurai tradition, once again seeing how masculinity was often associated with homoerotic relationships. So-called "ladyboys" have been present in Thai culture for centuries, and Thai kings openly took male and female lovers. In China homoerotic relationships were documented involving both sexes. Euphemisms such as "passions of the cut peach" are recorded since 600 BC. Opposition to homoerotic relationships arose around 600 to 900 AD, due to Muslim and Christian influences. You might be noting how much of the discussion focuses on male-male relationships, an occurrence not due to an absence of female-female erotic relationships, but because male events were recorded much better than those involving females. Consider that in ancient Greek society females were not even considered full citizens, and as such were to be penetrated along with slaves and pre-pubertal boys. However, female-female homoerotic relationships were recorded to some extent in ancient Chinese, Greek, Roman, and several other civilizations.

Present day Muslim society is generally very homophobic, with homoerotic contact carrying the death penalty in several nations such as Saudi Arabia, Iran, Mauritania, northern Nigeria, Sudan, and Yemen. In earlier times homoerotic relationships were much more acceptable in the region, despite the prevalence of the Muslim religion. For example, in Persia these relationships were openly practiced in many public settings, such as

176

taverns, military camps, coffee houses, bathhouses, monasteries, and seminaries. From 1501 to 1723 during the Safavid era, male houses of prostitution were legal and paid taxes. Same-sex erotic relationships are documented from northern India to the Western Sahara, many of the countries being Muslim. If not openly accepted, they were thinly veiled and not persecuted.

In other parts of the world homoerotic relationships were common and more socially acceptable, such as in the South Pacific and Americas pre-conquest. Throughout Melanesia same-sex erotic relationships have been an essential part of the social structure. Frequently, a young male pairs with an older male for a period of time as a form of initiation into adulthood, similar to the pattern in ancient Greek and Roman societies. In what is modern day Papua New Guinea these homoerotic relationships are still practiced, although with the intrusion of modern Western culture they are declining. In some instances the relationship ends and the person transitions into a heteroerotic relationship, while in others the homoerotic relationship continues over time, often along with heteroerotic relationships.

In the Americas region, the Aztecs, Mayans, Quechuas, Moches, Zapotecs, and Tupinamba of Brazil, practiced homoerotic behavior. Spanish conquerors horrified at the open practice of sodomy, initiated severe penalties including public executions, consisting of burning the sinful alive or having them being torn to pieces by dogs, all in the name of God. Hopefully, you get the idea that advancing conceptualizations of homoerotic relationships were really a regression, largely derived from repressive Christian and Muslim values. These values are more related than many followers would like to believe. Indeed, Christian, Muslim, and Jewish ideology is largely cut from the same cloth, and one that is generally very opposed to homoerotic behavior, or for that matter any non-procreative sexual act. We are the inheritors of this ideology, and hence it is not surprising that homoerotic behavior has a negative connotation. Except in a few of the more "civilized" enclaves it is still highly frowned upon. Even then such behavior often leads to discrimination, harassment, and assaults as we have seen.

Beyond the distant historical record, another way of examining the social construction of homoerotic behavior is to utilize a more modern day cross-cultural approach. We noted with the Spanish conquerors and peoples of the Americas how vast differences in perspective regarding homoerotic relationships can occur at one point in time. Ford and Beach in 1951 conducted a study using the Human Relations Area Files, a collection of research material on different societies. Of the 76 societies they examined, homoerotic behavior was socially acceptable and normal for certain people in 64%. They found it to be somewhat more frequent in adolescence, and practiced more by men than women. In certain societies homoerotic behavior was expected of young boys as part of initiation ceremonies. Within some settings the union of same-sex couples were formally recognized. From this classic study it is very evident that even in more modern times homoerotic behavior is considered normal in many societies, and certainly is not viewed as an aberration requiring explanation.

Age-structured homoerotic relationships, particularly between men and younger males, have been found to occur in contemporary societies in Africa, South America, and the South Pacific region. The region most studied is New Guinea. Research has revealed that age-structured homoerotic relationships between men and younger males is quite common, and typically occurs as part of initiation into adulthood. In an early work (1936)

Williams in Papuans Of The Trans-Fly described the "Bull-Roarer" ceremony of the Karaki. Young men were initiated into adulthood via passive anal sex performed on them by an older male. After a year the younger male would start to take the active role. Young men were not expected to practice these relationships for long, and were to partner with a female and have children. This transition to heteroerotic relationships was the norm.

The Sambia of highland New Guinea provide a fascinating and very well researched example of age-structured homoerotic relationships. Boys seven to ten years old undergo initiation into adulthood by engaging in homoerotic acts with older males. These unions induct them into ritual and military organizations. Oral sex is mostly practiced, and individuals take both the active and passive role. These homoerotic relationships transpire over a number of years, perhaps even a decade, until the man marries and has children when the behavior is expected to cease. Research reveals that in the vast majority of cases men make the transition from homoerotic to heteroerotic relationships. The Sambia are not unique given that 10-20% of South Pacific cultures approve of homoerotic contact between older and younger individuals.

A researcher who has studied the Sambia people extensively is Gilbert Herdt, who self-identifies as a homosexual male. In his book—Same Sex, Different Cultures—he describes the meshing of his own gay orientation with Sambia cultural beliefs. In spending much time with the Sambia he came to be highly trusted, and was allowed to ask about very personal aspects of sexual interests and behavior. Despite the cultural practice of homoerotic relationships, the Sambia could not understand how he led a "gay" life ongoing with a male partner. Some of the men he became closest to implored him to get married and have children, and even tried to arrange a marriage with a Sambian woman on more than one occasion. They felt sorry for him, and could not comprehend the concept of a "gay" lifestyle. There is no concept of homosexual or gay amongst the Sambia, although all males practice homoerotic relationships for years before transitioning to heteroerotic relationships.

Herdt summarizes the experience well by explaining, "Thus, it is remarkable for me to think that, even though living with the Sambia enabled me to accept in a way perhaps strange to the United States concept of same-sex relationships as normal and natural, the Sambia in their own way could only regard my own culture's identity constructs of homosexuality and gay as strange. Herein lies a powerful lesson about cross-cultural study of homosexuality—and a warning about the importance of being careful in the statements and assumptions we make about other people, as well as the need to respect their own customs for what they are—and are not." Herdt's statement underscores how the social construction of the same behavior can vary dramatically. Homoerotic behavior for the Sambia is considered a normal phase of development for males prior to marriage and children, while in the United States (and most of the modern world) is conceptualized as a permanent identity and real entity. The Sambia do not see homoerotic, or for that matter heteroerotic behavior, as a permanent dichotomous reality.

A key difference between Sambian and United States cultures is the prevalence of industrialization and urbanization in the latter. Herdt presents the notion that this very system of social organization might be an antecedent for "homosexuality" in the modern era, or in other words how we socially construct it. The example is given of young female silk factory workers in nineteenth

180

century Canton Delta China. Many of these woman formed erotic and economic bonds with each other that persisted, such that many never married men. China at the time was largely rural and male-dominated. Something about the shift to industrialization and urbanization contributed to these young women frequently forming lasting homoerotic relationships. It is likely that several variables contribute to this occurrence, some specific to the region and time. For example, many of these young women might have viewed the option of same-sex unions as a welcome relief from repression that would have ensued in a rural heterosexual marriage.

There are also reasons more general in nature for the link between how sexuality is socially constructed and industrialization/urbanization. One that seems evident from the discussion so far is the distinction between behavior (including mental events) and identity. Throughout much of time, and also in modern day settings not characterized by industrialization and urbanization, there appears to be more of a focus on behavior. Recall the long-standing notion of sodomites describing not a type of person, but a person who engaged in a particular behavior. By ceasing the behavior a person was no longer a sodomite. Behavior is the essential element and not identity.

In Sambian culture homoerotic and heteroerotic behavior is the focus, with appropriateness for males related to age. The same emphasis appears to have occurred in ancient Greek, Roman, and other cultures. Since many of these cultures were quite urban, perhaps the real issue is industrialization. It appears that with industrialization there is more of a focus on identity absent in non-industrial societies. Hence, if a person engages in a homoerotic relationship in our modern society, he or she is assumed to be a homosexual. The

181

homosexual identity is placed on the person. An individual who engages in erotic relationships with both sexes is given the bisexual identity. For the Sambia and ancient Greeks no such identity existed, the behavior itself not leading to a permanent categorization. As one researcher Jeffrey Weeks indicates, a distinction must be made "between homosexual behavior, which is universal, and a homosexual identity, which is historically specific."

Our modern day social construction of homoerotic relationships then appears to be one of establishing a permanent identity. Each of us absorbs the social prescription, and applies it automatically to our own behavior. Instead of viewing an instance of homoerotic behavior as simply that, it becomes an identity. The question arises as to what aspects of industrialization contribute to this focus on identity over behavior? There are many possible candidates and research needs to address this crucial topic. However, one that likely applies is defensive compensation for the lack of identity arising from industrialization.

Compensation is a fact of life, such as our immune system and natural reparative mechanisms compensating for infection and illness. Indeed, an absence or failure of compensation defines death. With industrialization people primarily serve to enhance productivity and economic growth, and as such are secondary. In ancient Greek and Sambian societies this notion would be ludicrous, given that people are most important. Ironically, even slaves in ancient Greece might be seen as more prominent than people in our era of industrialization. When people are prominent they feel important, hence there is no need to defensively compensate. With industrialization people lack this feeling and compensate by seeking meaningful identities. The permanent nature of the identities sought might result from how with industrial production nothing is permanent, other than the quest for endless economic growth. Essentially, people are placed in a position of being lesser than production and economic growth, and seek permanent identities to compensate. A homosexual or heterosexual identity, as opposed to homoerotic behavior, is one example of this defensive compensation. Sexual orientation identities provide a powerful in-group status and sense of belonging based on shared preferences, interests, beliefs, customs, and behavioral styles. Such identities can also help compensate for another aspect of industrialization, namely the isolation that many people experience as the family structure present in hunting-gathering and agricultural forms of social organization deteriorates.

Our modern day social construction of sexuality related to industrialization is then one of a permanent identity. Given its permanent nature, it is only naturally for it to be conceptualized into dichotomous homosexual and heterosexual categories. Based on the homosexual and heterosexual identities, bisexuality is more difficult to process. An interesting New York Times article by Carey in 2005—Straight, gay, or lying?: Bisexuality revisited— discussed how reluctant mainstream media is to accept bisexuality as a real sexual identity. The position of media aligns with the difficulty modern day society at large has in processing a dual identity. After all how can a person have two identities that seem discrete from one another? Breanne Fahs (Compulsory bisexuality?: The challenges of modern sexual fluidity) presents several ways that bisexuality has been constructed. It can be a permanent identity category, a trendy sexual identity, a transitory phase and hence not a true identity on the way to a real homosexual or heterosexual identity, or a chosen political and social identity not necessarily requiring actual sexual contact. Compare this to the fluid ease that Sambians and ancient Greeks work with homoerotic and heteroerotic behavior. When conceptualized in terms of behaviors instead of permanent identities, the problems in understanding bisexuality largely vanish.

So far we have seen how outside the context of our modern industrial era, homoerotic and heteroerotic behavior is not viewed as an identity. Conceptual and practical confusion occur when behavior is transformed into an identity. Crucial to the material presented throughout the book, is how a homosexual or heterosexual identity does not mesh ideally with the realities of our two dimensions of sexual orientation, heteroerotic and homoerotic. We all have the capacity, if not actual expression, for both derived from animal sexuality templates. But how can we have both, when we must have a homoerotic or heteroerotic identity? It is impossible, or at best, very awkward. No wonder people are so confused and anxious about sexuality in modern industrial society. Sexual orientation as an identity arguably represents the entire basis of psychoanalysis, with its focus on the sexual origin of neurosis. Essentially we have contributed to mental illness by how we have transformed sexuality from behavior to identity. Compare this to conceptualizing sexuality as two dimensions of homoerotic and heteroerotic, with appropriate behaviors flowing from both. We can then engage in both types of sexual expression with no conflict whatsoever, so long as we do not socially construct sexuality as identity.

A crucial issue is how our conceptualization of sexuality as an identity interacts with the homoerotic and heteroerotic dimensions. As a starting point, there must necessarily be friction and tension. Most people have some significant value on both dimensions, and conceivably there is no such thing as a true zero value on either dimension, although objective research is required in this regard. Let us take the example of a person with a higher heteroerotic motivation and lower homoerotic motivation, who identifies as heterosexual. What happens if this person enters a setting, such as a prison, that traditionally activates the homoerotic dimension to assist in alliance formation or provide other benefits, even sexual release or emotional closeness? Activation of the homoerotic dimension will produce confusion and mental distress in many individuals, because it conflicts with the heterosexual identity. The person might unconsciously or even consciously suppress the homoerotic motivation, thereby deactivating the dimension. Perhaps the person will act on it, and have to struggle with the possibility that he or she has a "bisexual" identity. Worse, if fixated on an either/or sexual identity, the person might worry about being "homosexual," only to discover that heterosexual functioning is fine away from prison. Talk about confusing!

Let us take another example, this time of a person who is higher in homoerotic than heteroerotic motivation identifying with being homosexual. What happens when this person desires having children? The desire will activate the heteroerotic dimension, but conflict with the homosexual identity will produce confusion and anxiety. Once again the person might consider the possibility of being "bisexual," but have trouble with this notion given how in a dichotomized sexual identity world it is difficult to process. The person might unconsciously or consciously suppress the heteroerotic motivation denying the desire for children, thereby deactivating the heteroerotic dimension. Either way there is a struggle, and some significant mental processing. If a person engages in actions consistent with the sexual dimension, but inconsistent with their sexual identity—homoerotic if a heterosexual identity and heteroerotic if a homoerotic

185

identity—then guilt and self-criticism often arises, reinforced in many instances by input from friends and family members. No wonder we are highly neurotic compared to many people in more traditional societies. Out of the confusion and resulting frustration, anger often ensues that is likely a key factor in the widespread discrimination, harassment, and assaults against people perceived as being homosexual or bisexual.

The question arises as to why those identifying as "homosexual" do not persecute heterosexuals? A key reason is the secondary status of being homosexual. Given the evolutionary significance of reproduction, a homosexual identity is socially constructed as lesser than. In societies emphasizing sexual behavior and not sexual identities, both homoerotic and heteroerotic behavior serve important functions, and the former does not preclude reproduction. In fact in some settings, homoerotic behavior even enhances the chances of acquiring a mate, or higher status mate, based on the benefits of forming an alliance with a higher-ranking same-sex individual. There is then no conflict at all between homoerotic behavior and reproduction. On the other hand, a homoerotic sexual identity must necessarily have a secondary status, because for the most part it precludes reproduction. In addition, due to the importance of reproduction to evolutionary fitness the average level of hetererotic motivation is almost certainly higher than homoerotic motivation, resulting in most people identifying with being heterosexual, thereby making this the dominant sexual orientation identity group. The insecurity derived from the secondary status of homosexuality and its lower prevalence, likely accounts for the lesser frequency of discrimination, harassment, and assault perpetrated by homosexuals against heterosexuals.

The secondary status of homosexuality also provides another reason why most people identify with being heterosexual—It discourages people from identifying with being homosexual. Hence, only those with a very low heteroerotic motivation and high homoerotic motivation will identify as being "homosexual." The much higher homoerotic over heteroerotic motivation makes any other option untenable, although some opt for a bisexual identity. However, the difficulty encountered in understanding bisexuality in a dichotomized world makes the status of this sexual orientation type uncertain. Anyone with a substantial level of heteroerotic motivation will identify with being "heterosexual," given its higher status and unambiguous nature.

A social construction of sexuality more consistent with our two-dimensional sexual nature, resolves any problems that arise when sexuality becomes an identity. Both homoerotic and heteroerotic behavior is prescribed, in line with the practices of the particular culture. Since both are expressed reproduction is not a concern at all. Even shifting from one to the other, commonly early homoerotic to later heteroerotic, appears quite seamless for most individuals. There are instances of people in these cultures preferring same-sex relationships, but they do not identify with being homosexual. Perhaps a high homoerotic motivation, combined with a low heteroerotic motivation, makes it challenging for the person to routinely function in fully heterosexual relationships. However, given that historical and more contemporary examples align with non-zero values on both dimensions, some capacity to engage in heteroerotic and homoerotic behavior does seem to exist in each person. When people are forced to identify with a heterosexual or homosexual orientation, lower levels of motivation on the non-dominant dimension are suppressed and deactivated.

Higher values are much harder to ignore, and are then more likely to be expressed and recognized as a bisexual orientation.

As presented in the chapter on dimension activation, in some instances sexual abuse and mental illness likely deactivate a dimension, making it appear that the person has zero motivation, when there is actually a low but positive value. In an evolutionary context with the social advantages of alliance formation, tension reduction, and reconciliation derived from homoerotic behavior, a person with a true zero motivation would likely have been at a major disadvantage, much as with our close cousins the bonobos. Such an individual would try to secure reproductive opportunities without support, ensuring the wrath of higher-ranking same-sex individuals, and would have no real way to ease the resulting tensions and reconcile with the aggressor/s. Conceivably, individuals with zero homoerotic motivation would be at such a disadvantage, from a reproductive perspective, that genes favoring it would vanish from the gene pool, or only persist at a low frequency.

The social construction of human sexual orientation most consistent with our nature is then one emphasizing both homoerotic and heteroerotic behavior, without any reference to identity. This is a general social construction that can be seen as generic and applying to all people over time. More specific aspects of the social construction are tailored to the given culture. Considering how homogenized the world currently is with globalization of the economy, it is difficult to see how a shift to this type of social construction will ever occur naturally. Indeed, if it truly is the case that we are relying on sexual orientation identities to compensate for our secondary status within industrial society, then the dichotomous heterosexual and homosexual identities will

188

almost certainly persist. Change to a more adaptive and less anxiety inducing social construction of sexuality, will only occur if we counter the social prescriptions linked to industrialization by focusing on behavior, and not identity, consistent with our natural homoerotic and heteroerotic capacities.

In addition to resolving the inner confusion and turmoil commonly experienced, a motivation for such a shift is to help end the discrimination against homosexuals, bisexuals and transgender people. Sexual orientation socially constructed as an identity, fosters in-group/out-group distinctions, fueling discrimination. A natural component of our social cognition is to distinguish in-group from out-group members. This propensity almost certainly derives from our evolution in hunting-gathering groups, where in-group members shared genes. Consequently, altruistic behavior helped pass on the helper's genes (so-called kin selection). Out-group members being genetically unrelated could not be trusted, as they might seek group resources, including reproductively active females. Helping such individuals was wasted energy from the perspective of evolutionary fitness, unless a reciprocation of behavior occurred. Whatever the precise origin, we naturally separate people into those belonging to our in-group and those in the out-group. Various criteria can be applied to separate in-group from out-group members, such as skin color, membership in a club, ideology, team affiliation, and identity; the list can be quite endless. If sexual orientation consists of homoerotic and heteroerotic dimensions present in each of us, using sexual orientation as a guide to in-group/out-group status is meaningless. How can you perceive someone as being out-group when both of you have the same traits? In a sense then everyone is in-group!

Separate homosexual and heterosexual identities fit very well with in-group and out-group distinctions. If you identify as homosexual, then fellow homosexuals are in-group, and heterosexuals are members of the out-group. On the other hand, if you identify with being heterosexual, then homosexuals are out-group and heterosexuals in-group. Once this categorization occurs discrimination follows. Members of the in-group are automatically credited with certain positive traits, while out-group members are viewed as being inferior. Research, such as by Brewer & Miller (Intergroup relations), have found that people apply more positive evaluations to characteristics of the in-group that distinguish it from the out-group, thereby exaggerating the between group differences. Once membership status is conferred, people tend to adopt the predominant beliefs, attitudes, and behavioral style of the in-group. Other researchers such as Reynolds and colleagues (When are we better than them and they worse than us? A closer look at social discrimination in positive and negative domains) have found that out-group members are often looked down on and discriminated against.

In a classic in-group/out-group project known as Robbers Cave, Sherif (Intergroup Conflict And Cooperation: The Robbers Cave Experiment) studied eleven-year old boys arriving at summer camp. The boys were immediately separated into two groups. For the first week they were kept apart and encouraged to engage in cooperative activities designed to strengthen in-group identification. The experimenters had each group select their own name to emphasize uniqueness. When the Rattlers and Eagles were allowed to interact antagonism and hostility immediately ensued, consisting of name-calling, fights, camp raids at night, and competition for places in meal line-ups. This pronounced antagonism transpired despite the fact that members of both groups were identical in terms of age, race, socioeconomic background, physical attributes, and psychological stability. Members of the in-group were favored, and those in the out-group were viewed with enough disdain to generate heated conflict. The resentment was so great that they even forfeited pleasurable activities, such as movies, if it meant being in the presence of the other group. Simply bringing the Rattlers and Eagles together had no appreciably positive effect; in fact, it increased competition. The only intervention that significantly decreased hostility consisted of challenging tasks requiring the combined efforts of both groups.

If nearly identical individuals can show so much hostility to each other, just based on an arbitrary in-group/out-group classification, then it follows that distinctions based on more permanent identities can produce pronounced discrimination, bias, and hostility. Hostility towards homosexuals often seems to occur in those who are uncertain about their own sexual orientation, or status as a heterosexual when framed in terms of sexual orientation as an identity. Of course as we have seen, heterosexual and homosexual identities are only a social construct, and hence doubts are understandable. An interesting finding from in-group/out-group research linking uncertainties about a person's own heterosexual identity to discrimination against the homosexual out-group, is that a peripheral in-group status can produce more negative behavior towards the out-group than is demonstrated by core members of the in-group. For example, Noel and colleagues (Peripheral ingroup membership status and public negativity towards outgroups) found that pledge members of fraternities and sororities, applied more coercive persuasion strategies against out-group members than did established in-group members, apparently to impress core members regarding their standing. However, even those with confidence in their status within the in-group tend to be biased against out-group members simply based on group identification. Hence, it is understandable that if a person identifies with being heterosexual they will naturally have a bias against the homosexual out-group. This occurrence does not justify the behavior; instead it reflects the influence of in-group/out-group distinctions on our social cognition, and provides a strong motivation for transforming sexual orientation back into behaviors that we all have the capacity for instead of an identity.

Social construction represents the fourth component of sexual orientation, the others consisting of dimensions of sexual orientation (homoerotic and heteroerotic), activation of these dimensions, and erotic fantasy. It guides how sexual orientation is understood, expressed, and responded to. Although we tend to view ourselves as more enlightened and advanced than people from earlier times, and those in more modern day South Pacific tribal societies, this perspective is difficult to support. With the advent of industrialization, and the secondary status of people relative to production, we have created sexual orientation identities that only partially align with our true homoerotic and heteroerotic motivations. Behaviors have been transformed into identities only approximating the realities of sexual orientation, and ones fostering a great deal on inner confusion, frustration, and neurosis, plus outwardly directed discrimination and hostility. We have regressed instead of progressed. By rewriting the social construction of sexual orientation to align it with our true nature, we will greatly reduce both our inner struggles and outwardly directed antagonism. This rewrite must involve transforming identities back into homoerotic and heteroerotic behaviors.

TRANSGENDER

Transgender occurs in ever country and region of the world, and although the expression is similar the acceptance and meaning varies. On the Indian subcontinent a third gender known as "hijra" in Hindi is said to exist. Effeminate gay men and male-to-female transgender people are grouped as "kathoey" in Thailand and Laos. In Polynesian culture there is a traditional status for transgender people, known as "mahu." North American First Nations people have traditionally believed in more than two genders, the third designation known as "two-spirit" people (formerly bedarche). Throughout recorded time transgender has occurred, as with male-to-female people being recognized in ancient Islamic culture, and the Gallae of ancient Rome who undertook self-castration. Transgender is then part of who we are as a species, because it derives from a very human-specific psychological occurrence—Gender identity.

The inner sense of being male or female constitutes gender identity. People often assume that "homosexuals" possess the gender identity of the opposite biological sex, with gay men being effeminate and lesbians masculine. However, the majority of those identifying with a homosexual orientation have a gender identity that aligns with their biological sex, determined by genetics and also primary and secondary sexual characteristics. Genetically, males have one X and one Y chromosome, and females XX. Primary sexual characteristics are those vital to being male or female, such as a penis or vagina and associated reproductive structures. Secondary sexual characteristics are ones such as the amount and distribution of body hair

194

and deepness of voice. People who identify with being homosexual are just like the majority of people identifying as heterosexual, their gender identity aligning with their biological sex. But what happens when a person's sense of being male or female does not align with biological sex? Then we have what is known as transgender, the trans referring to a shift of gender identity from that aligning with biological sex.

Highlighting how well gender identity typically aligns with biological sex, enormous confusion and misunderstanding occurs when there is misalignment. Consequently, transgender individuals are often rejected by others and society at large. In the discrimination chapter we learned how tough it is for those identifying with being homosexual. Transgender individuals experience at least as much discrimination and hostility, and in some instances more. For example, in the EU LGBT survey more transgender people reported discrimination when looking for a job or at work then did homosexuals and bisexuals. Serious physical attacks are also not uncommon, as evidenced by the following examples. On June 16, 2001, 18-year old Shaun Murphy bludgeoned to death Fred Martinez, a transgender student in Colorado. Murphy bragged about attacking a "fag." Terrianne Summers, a 51-year old transgender woman and activist for transgender rights, was shot and killed in her front yard in Florida, on December 12, 2002. No arrests were made and her murder was not investigated as a hate crime. In February of 2008, Duanna Johnson, a transgender woman, was beaten by a police officer while held in the Shelby County Criminal Justice Center in Tennessee. Johnson claimed that officers called her "faggot' and "he-she" prior to and during the incident. Later that year she was shot and killed by three unknown assailants. On September 11, 2010, Victoria Carmen

White, a 28-year old black transgender woman was shot to death in her New Jersey apartment. Her killer, Alrashim Chambers, is believed to have targeted her due to her being transgender. Chrissy Lee Polis, a 22-year old transgender woman, received a severe beating by two women triggering a seizure. The beating occurred when Polis entered a woman's bathroom in Baltimore County, Maryland. A McDonald's employee filmed the encounter and released it on the Internet.

Not surprisingly transgender people suffer from high rates of depression and anxiety with suicidal behavior not being uncommon. The term gender dysphoria captures the negative mood and behavioral state of many with gender identity issues. In the Diagnostic and Statistical Manual 5 (DSM-5), widely used by psychiatrists and clinical psychologists, gender dysphoria has replaced Gender Identity Disorder. The basic notion is that when experienced gender does not align with biological sex, a person often suffers emotionally and behaviorally, such that there is significant distress and impairment in functioning. Gender dysphoria is far more common in children than in adults. Research, such as that by Zucker and Bradley (Gender identity disorder and psychosexual problems in children and adolescents) shows that even in children with a strong desire to be the opposite sex, only a small percentage will continue to experience gender dysphoria. Hence, most of those uncertain about their gender identity in childhood grow out of it so to speak. However, the longer the sense of being in the wrong body persists throughout childhood and adolescence, the more likely it is to constitute a permanent scenario. But why would there ever be misalignment between male/female biological sex and the sense of being male or female?

Causation debates typically take the form of social/psychological versus biological, as we noted regarding sexual orientation. Transgender is no exception to this trend. Representing the former is sexologist John Money and followers, with the perspective that there is failure to socialize into the correct gender during childhood and adolescence, leading to gender identity problems and mental health issues. A strong critic of John Money, and a transgender woman (male-to-female), Lynn Conway, believes that Money used his dominant status in the niche field of sexology to elevate his "genitalia and upbringing" theory. It is alleged that he fabricated many results, and concealed evidence that countered his theories. Money's approach formed the basis of arbitrary surgical sex reassignments of infants with ambiguous genitalia, mostly boys with small or missing penises. The basic concept being that if a child is socialized to the surgically assigned sex, all will be well. Unfortunately, all was not well, and many boys reassigned as girls later wanted to become boys when a male gender identity emerged. However, they lost what male genital tissue they had, and the capacity to achieve orgasm. Not the greatest end result to say the least.

Representing another behavioral theory of transgender is that of sexologist, Ray Blanchard. His theory exclusively focuses on male-to-female transgender. Kurt Freund, and colleagues Steiner and Chan, distinguished two types of cross-gender identity in 1982, "homosexual transsexuals," who are sexually attracted to men and "heterosexual transsexuals," who are aroused by the idea of having a female body but want a female partner. During the 1980's and 1990's Blanchard built on this work, proposing that "homosexual transsexuals" transition because they are attracted to men. Non-homosexual transsexuals Blanchard refers to as autogynephilic; auto self and gynephelia love of oneself as a woman. To digress, a general comment, appropriate at this point, that I strongly feel needs to be considered by the entire gender identity area is the problem of terminology. No other area of social and scientific study is characterized by such a bewildering array of terms— Autogynephilic, trans-man, trans-woman, cisgender, transsexual, transvestite, androgyne, gender queer, bigender, drag queen, faux queen and the list goes on and on. There are said to be about 40 different transgender states.

The confusing array of terms makes it virtually impossible for the average person, or perhaps anyone without a PhD in sexology, to understand the area. A new mental health condition that I suggest be called, Gender Identity Terminology Disorder, needs to be recognized. Symptoms include mental confusion, dysphoria, anxiety, agitation, and the feeling of being mentally overwhelmed, upon being exposed to gender identity terminology. As a medical practitioner and theoretical researcher, I have learned to keep terminology basic to facilitate communication. Niche areas, such as sexology, often protect their turf by producing a separate language of sorts that is difficult for outsiders to acquire and become proficient in. The terminology confusion both reflects and adds to the confusion encountered with transgender issues, for those experiencing it and others trying to understand it.

Getting back to Blanchard's autogynephilic transgender type from the digression into terminology, he proposed that sexual arousal at the thought of being a woman motivates some male-to-female transsexuals to transition. Blanchard's theory has been intensely criticized, and now Blanchard appears to see these two types as descriptors instead of causes. Charles Moser, a

198

physician, rejects Blanchard's theory, indicating that it lacks supporting data and fails to account for many of the sexual and romantic interests of transgender people. Julia Serano, a biochemist and "trans-activist," points out methodological flaws in the research, such as overlapping study populations limited to the Clark Institute of Psychiatry in Toronto, and confusing correlation for causation. Regarding the latter, Blanchard assumes that sexual arousal at the thought of being a woman motivates a man to transition, but is it not more likely that the person feels like a woman (transgender) and then feels the arousal of a woman? Ultimately, though, the demise of social/psychological theories comes from the strength of biological causation data.

Biological factors influencing transgender began to be seriously considered with the work of Harry Benjamin, a physician who at the request of Alfred Kinsey started treating people with these issues. His work began in the late 1940's and continued through the era dominated by the social/psychological, and largely behaviorist views, of Money and Blanchard. Benjamin began using hormonal treatments, and his strategy shifted thinking towards the perspective that hormonal release during pregnancy influences brain development associated with gender identity. A study conducted by Zhou and colleagues, working at the Netherlands Institute For Brain Research (A sex difference in the human brain and its relationship to transsexuality) is crucial to consider. Research transpired over an 11-year period, and focused on transgender individuals and non-transgender control male and females, who donated their brains for study upon death. The researchers discovered that male and female brains differ in the size of an area linked to sexual functioning—The central bed nucleus of the stria terminalis (BSTc), being about 62% larger in normal males brains. The male-to-female transgender individuals showed BSTc sizes like those of females, and female-to-male subjects BSTc sizes similar to males. The possibility exists that hormonal treatments could have produced this result, but this option was ruled out because some of the non-transgender male and female controls had received other-sex hormones for medical conditions, thereby providing a comparison group. The impact of removal of the testes in male-to-female transgender subjects was also ruled out as a reason for the results found.

Zhou and colleagues concluded that brain development in-utero (in the womb) accounted for the results. It is important to appreciate that the focus is on gender identity, and not sexual orientation, as there is no consistent evidence that brain development impacts on the latter, other than perhaps influencing the strength of a person's homoerotic and heteroerotic motivations. An important followup study was conducted by Frank Kruijver and colleagues (Male-to-female transsexuals have female neuron numbers in a limbic nucleus), also of the Netherlands Institute For Brain Research, this time focusing on the number of neurons in the BSTc, and not BSTc volume, as did Zhou and colleagues. Their results supported that of Zhou, finding that normal male brains have twice as many neurons in the BSTc as do female brains, and that male-to-female transgender individuals show the female pattern. The researchers indicated that hormone treatments and sex hormone level variations in adulthood did not seem to influence the BSTc neuron cell numbers. Research by Chung and colleagues (Sexual differentiation of the bed nucleus of the stria terminalis in humans may extend into adulthood), revealed that sexual dimorphism (variation between sexes) does not actually become established until adulthood. The researchers speculate that fetal hormone levels produce changes in the BSTc that later result in the size and cell number changes noted by Zhou and Kruijver, or that these changes in the BSTc occur due to failure to develop a gender identity consistent with biological sex.

Similar differences between males and females and transgender individuals have been found for other brain regions linked to sexuality. For example, Garcia-Falgueras and Swabb (A sex difference in the hypothalamic uncinate nucleus: Relationship to gender identity) examined the interstial nucleus of the anterior hypothalamus (INAH-3) that we also looked at in regards to sexual orientation. As with the BSTc results, males show larger INAH-3 volumes by a factor of 1.9, and 2.3 times the cell number than females, with male-to-female transgender subjects showing the female pattern, and female-to-male subjects the male pattern, the results not being due to hormone exposure. Combined the brain research strongly suggest that transgender individuals have differences in brain region size and cell number consistent with the sex they feel they are, and other than their biological sex.

The story does not end with the brain alterations during fetal development, because genes appear to play a role as well with several linked to the development of male/female brain differences, at least in animal models. Focusing on human subjects, Hare and colleagues (Androgen receptor repeat length polymorphism associated with male-to-female transsexualism) found that male-to-female transgender individuals have longer repeat lengths of a gene influencing the androgen receptor (NR3C4). Longer repeat lengths reduce the ability of this receptor to bind the male hormone testosterone. This finding reveals at least one way that sex-based brain differences and gene influences might interact with each other—The brain is initially set up to be female, but with the presence of a Y (male) chromosome testosterone "washes" the brain at a critical period, producing changes in sex-linked structures resulting in male brain development; however, if receptors for testosterone cannot properly bind the hormone, then brain development might proceed along female lines, despite biological sex being male. In the case of female-to-male transgender, the developing brain might receive a male hormone "wash" at a critical period, due to excessive male hormone levels, with genes potentially influencing this occurrence. A variant of a gene (CYP17) that acts on the sex hormones pregnenolone and progesterone, has been associated with female-to-male transgender.

UNDERSTANDING THE NATURE OF TRANSGENDER:

Masculinity/Femininity & Gender Identity:

So far we have seen how hormones in combination with genetic influences guide the brains of some males to a female pattern, and the reverse for some females, contributing to transgender, but we do not really have a feel for how these changes express themselves. The discussion makes it seem that gender identity is either/or, male or female, but as we have learned discrete entities are an illusion our brain prefers. Continuums characterize nature and this applies to masculinity/femininity, as we saw in the Dimensions Of Sexual Orientation chapter. As discussed in that chapter, there are a variety of traits related to masculinity and femininity, as presented by Michael Shively and John De Cocco in their 2010 article, Components of sexual identity. These include:

Physical attributes—Consists of secondary sexual characteristics such as presence or absence of body hair.

Physical condition—Healthy men and women are seen as being more masculine and feminine, respectively. Average weight women are viewed as more feminine, than very overweight or too thin women.

Mannerisms—Refers to how an individual moves, sits, or stands. More uncontrolled hand movements increase the perception of femininity.

Adornment—What a person selects to put on including tattoos, jewelry, and clothing.

Personality traits—Masculinity is often associated with aggression, assertiveness, and confidence, whereas femininity is typically linked to nurturance and softness.

Grooming—Men and women are seen as being more masculine and feminine, respectively, when they are well kept in terms of clothing and hair.

Speech and vocabulary—Consists of voice inflection including pitch and tone, and also the words used in speech with slang seen as more masculine.

Social interaction—How a person relates to others in social situations, with more dominant and in control behavior typically being viewed as masculine.

Interests—Some activities are seen as more traditionally masculine, such as team sports and others such as opera more feminine.

Habits—These diverse and specific behaviors include nail biting, seen as more feminine, and cigar smoking considered to be more masculine.

With such an extensive range of masculine and feminine traits, it is impossible for someone to be fully masculine and not at all feminine, or the reverse. We learned how one dimension ranging from masculine to feminine does not work, because these traits must trade off such that masculine people cannot be at all feminine, and feminine people not at all masculine. We demonstrate a mixture of feminine and masculine traits, an occurrence supporting separate dimensions for masculinity and femininity, given that with separate dimensions these traits do not trade off against each other. Hence, genes and brain development, either in isolation or in combination, promote a mixture of masculine and feminine traits in each person. With an intact system, the male XY chromosome pattern provides an appropriately timed male hormone "wash" of the brain during fetal development, favoring more masculine than feminine traits. Consequently, a more masculine pattern emerges aligning with male biological sex. The XX female pattern in an intact system blocks this male hormone "wash," favoring more feminine than masculine traits, in line with female biological sex. When masculine traits significantly exceed feminine traits a male gender identity typically emerges, and when feminine traits substantially exceed masculine ones, a female gender identity usually emerges.

Gender Identity & Transgender:

Consistent with the notion of continuums, and also the messiness and imperfection of life, the ideal intact system does not always transpire. For the most part, gender identity aligns with biological sex, such that both "heterosexual" and "homosexual" males typically identify with being male, and female "heterosexuals" and "homosexuals" identify with being female. However, when this does not manifest transgender issues are present. Most of those falling outside the norm of gender identity aligning with biological sex, have a fairly even mix of masculine and feminine traits, and adopt a dual (or neither) gender identity, although they might not see it in exactly this way. The terms "gender-queer" and

204

androgyne (meaning both or neither sex) have been applied, but as mentioned these terms tend to add to and not detract from the confusion and misunderstanding. The notion of a dual gender identity surprises some people, because given our predilection to see discrete entities, we prefer to believe that if someone has any transgender identity it must be opposite to their biological sex. However, with nature organized dimensionally there is understandably a continuum of gender identities from masculine to feminine, with an approximately equal number of masculine and feminine traits on these two dimensions favoring a dual (or neither) identity. Only a limited number of transgender individuals have a single gender identity other than their biological sex, likely due to sex-linked brain structures developing opposite to biological sex.

Now you might be thinking, "Even though it's somewhat confusing it does make sense, but what are the practical implications?" The conceptual nature of transgender ties in very nicely with practical applications, and can help all of us understand human sexuality in a much more enlightened fashion. For instance, when people encounter an effeminate male child, teenager, or adult, the automatic response is, "That person is gay." Frequently this notion is so strongly believed that no other option is considered. With our enlightened understanding of gender identity, we can now see how this automatic assumption is wrong, dead wrong! First, as we have learned there is no definitive association between masculinity/femininity and sexual orientation. Hence, the individual demonstrating traits other than their biological sex is transgender, not gay! So a biological male with highly feminine traits likely has a female gender identity. Now here is where the really interesting part comes in, and one that many people including sexology researchers fail to appreciate—If the transgender male-to female is attracted to males, that person is heterosexual! A person with a female gender identity who is attracted to men is not at all "gay." You might say, "Doesn't biological sex count?" Our mind is what makes us human, and perceptions are everything to us. Gender identity is what counts, as simple as that. So when you encounter a highly feminine male or highly masculine female, it is best to assume that the individual has a gender identity other than their biological sex, and base homosexual and heterosexual categorizations (to the extent they apply) on gender identity.

Consider the two-type transgender described by Freund and Blanchard, with "homosexual" and "heterosexual" transsexuals. "Homosexual" transsexual males are attracted to males, and this presumably motivates them to transition. Completely the opposite applies—The person identifies with being female, hence the desire to transition, with the combination of a female gender identity and attraction to males making the person "heterosexual." On the other hand, heterosexual transgender males (autogynephilic), who are drawn to women, are actually "homosexual," because if they truly have a female gender identity then attraction to females is homosexual in orientation. So our conceptual reasoning pertaining to gender identity and sexuality has the very practical application of correcting flawed perspectives, that can fuel misunderstanding and discrimination against transgender people, and also reduce their self-acceptance.

How do the all-important dimensions of homoerotic and heteroerotic behavior fit into this enlightened understanding? We learned that each of us have separate homoerotic and heteroerotic dimensions providing the capacity for same-sex and other-sex sexual behaviors. Note that I did not say orientations. To

206

properly interface these dimensions with gender identity, we simply relate the homoerotic dimension to the sex consistent with gender identity, and the heteroerotic dimension to the sex other than gender identity. In other words, we anchor homoerotic and heteroerotic motivations to gender identity. Hence, when a person identifies with being female, regardless of biological sex, the homoerotic dimension applies to sexual behaviors involving females, and the heteroerotic dimension to sexual behaviors with males. When a person identifies with being male, regardless of biological sex, the homoerotic dimension applies to sexual behaviors involving males, and the heteroerotic dimension to sexual behaviors with females. A male-to-female transgender individual is activating the homoerotic dimension when sexual behavior with a female occurs, and the heteroerotic dimension when sexual acts with males take place. This might seem somewhat confusing, but if we just flip or rotate the standard thinking 180 degrees it all becomes clear—The power of solid conceptual reasoning demonstrated. If you follow it you are actually ahead of many sexologists in your understanding.

In the event of a dual gender identity, or neither, the terms homoerotic and heteroerotic breakdown, although the person still has the two sexual orientation dimensions facilitating attraction for and/or sexual behavior directed towards males and females. At the risk of further adding to gender terminology confusion, a potential option in the event of a dual gender identity, is bierotic, as it describes attraction and/or sexual behavior directed towards both males and females, anchored in a gender identity that is both feminine and masculine. This term would not be applicable to bisexuals who identify either with being male or female, but only to those who have a dual gender identity.

INTERSEX CONDITIONS:

Detracting somewhat from the elegant simplicity derived from our enlightened understanding of gender identity, and how it relates to sexual attraction, some people are born, or in rare cases later acquire, biological sexual characteristics that are indeterminate or mixed. These so-called intersex conditions occur in approximately 1 in 4,500 births, with about 15 recognized types. Most of these involve XY chromosomes coding for males. With intersex conditions there is understandably much more gender confusion and dysphoria relative to the general population. One of the more common intersex conditions is complete androgen insensitivity syndrome, involving XY chromosomes and testes producing testosterone, but full insensitivity to androgens. Consequently, the individual is born with female or ambiguous genitalia and is typically reared female. Most end up developing a female gender identity.

Intersex conditions also occur when chromosomes code for a female (XX). The most common of these is congenital adrenal hyperplasia, involving excess production from the adrenal gland of male hormones in the developing fetus, due to a deficiency of certain enzymes. Exposure to high levels of androgens from other sources, such as hormonal drug treatment of the mother, can produce similar outcomes to congenital adrenal hyperplasia. Despite the two X chromosomes, females with this condition (or exposure to high androgens from the mother) experience the male hormone "wash" during fetal development, leading to masculine traits. These individuals often engage in tomboyish behavior, but of course not all "tomboys" suffer from congenital adrenal hyperplasia. Although male hormone levels definitely play a role in the development of masculine and feminine traits and gender identity, lower than normal androgen exposure in males does not always compromise male gender identity, nor does higher androgen exposure in females always jeopardize female gender identity. This occurrence suggests that genetic factors unrelated to male/female hormones, and possibly as yet undiscovered environmental influences, also play a significant role in the development of gender identity.

When hormonal influences are inconsistent with chromosomal sex and biological sex is intermediate, gender identity naturally tends to be more variable. In a truly discrete universe there would be only biological males and females without any intersex, but in a continuous world some degree of mixing is normal. For example, there are males with very little body and facial hair but deep masculine voices, and females with quite a bit of body and facial hair but feminine voices. Alterations in male sex hormone levels, and the way they act during fetal development, contribute to a mixing of masculine and feminine characteristics. Hence, with intersex conditions gender identity issues are almost certain, but how and when to intervene in the context of these conditions, and also when biological sex is non-ambiguous but gender is other than biological sex?

INTERVENTIONS:

To intervene or not intervene, that is the question. Given the emotional discomfort that often comes with transgender, some form of treatment is typically required, but not always, and timing is a crucial consideration. An important starting point is whether or not intersex issues apply. The treatment of intersex conditions is complex, and best left to specialty medical clinics having a lot of experience with these young individuals. Experience counts generally and certainly when it comes to surgical, hormonal, and psychosocial interventions for youth with intersex issues. The old behavioral notion advocated by Money that children can simply be socialized to become a given sex certainly does not apply, and many earlier surgical interventions based on this notion had devastating consequences, manifesting during adolescence when gender identity opposite to surgical assignment emerged. Intervention involves careful selection and comprehensive surgical, hormonal, and psychosocial management.

Regarding outcomes of interventions for intersex conditions, Greenfield and colleagues conducted an informative study—Management of children with ambiguous genitalia using a "disorders of sex development (DSD) team." 14 patients treated between 1985 and 2008 for various intersex conditions were followed for an average of 12.5 years to assess outcome. 8 children were assigned and reared as girls, and 6 as boys. 3 with congenital adrenal hyperplasia were reared as girls, all having hormonal treatment, 2 underwent surgery with 1 involving clitoris reduction and another reconstruction of the vagina (vaginoplasty). The 1 child with androgen insensitivity syndrome was reared as female. 4 of the children had what is known as gonadal dysgenesis, a condition where the reproductive structures are underdeveloped and dysfunctional, mainly consisting of fibrotic tissue. All 4 were assigned as boys with surgical removal of female reproductive tissue, and also correction of the penis such that urine exits in the proper location (hypospadias repair). 4 of the intersex children were true hermaphrodites, meaning born with both male (testicular) and female (ovarian) reproductive tissue, although both types of tissue never function in the same individual. 3 of these children were assigned as boys and had surgical correction of the penis, combined with removal of any female reproductive tissue. The other true hermaphrodite was assigned as a girl, and placed on estrogen with surgical vaginal dilation. Follow-up of these individuals showed that gender identity consistent with the gender assigned occurred in all cases, and no gender dysphoria arose.

Based on the results of Greenfield and colleagues, it certainly appears that assignment of intersex individuals by an expert treatment team works very well. However, with so many things in life there are always pluses and minuses. On the plus side of the equation, is how an intersex individual undergoing strategic surgical and hormonal interventions can have their gender identity and biological sex align with each other. Consequently, gender dysphoria is greatly reduced or prevented. On the negative side, there remains the possibility that the person will develop a gender identity inconsistent with the sex of assignment, and experience great distress from this, particularly when the assignment is made during infancy or childhood. Perhaps of greater concern, even when an expert treatment team determines assignment and provides comprehensive treatment, are risks associated with surgery. Often surgeons and those advocating for surgery downplay the risks, but they are not to be underestimated with any surgery. There is always the risk of chronic pain syndromes, greatly reducing the quality of life and leaving people vulnerable to narcotic addiction.

More relevant to intersex surgery itself, is the need for ongoing surgery as highlighted by Jean Calleja-Aguis and colleagues in their paper—A review of the management of intersex. They indicate that surgical reconstruction carried out in infancy often needs to be revised in puberty. In regards to vaginoplasty, they point to surgical results indicating that 36-100% of women report vaginal stenosis (narrowing) requiring repeat surgery, and with repeat surgery the risk of further complications increases. Calleja-Agius and colleagues also indicate that leaving surgical repair of intersex conditions until later, allows for the input of the person as to what sex they wish assignment to. Hormones if involved in the reassignment have to be taken for the life of the person, often a problem as people tend not to persist with drug treatments, such as during the rebellious years of adolescence, and the hormones can have medical complications. Clearly there are pluses and minuses to medical intervention for intersex conditions and also to the timing of it, that further experience might help resolve.

In the instance of non-intersex transgender there are other considerations. A key one being the degree of "trans" involved. As mentioned, in many instances when gender identity does not fully align with biological sex, the individual appears to indentify with both genders, or in some cases neither. For these individuals many options are applicable, and often no surgical or hormonal intervention is required. A key aspect is self-acceptance, starting with the realization that due to hormonal and genetic influences during fetal brain development, acting either in isolation or combination, they have a balance of masculine and feminine traits often resulting in gender confusion and dysphoria, and the feeling that they are both genders, or possibly neither. A positive spin is that they are actually in a stronger position than most people, because they have a greater capacity to see the world from a balanced perspective, characterized by a blend of masculine and feminine traits. Although this sounds great many of these individuals experience substantial emotional pain, made worse by the rejection they often encounter from others. If the larger society acquires the enlightened understanding provided here, then hopefully

212

rejection and discrimination will be reduced and replaced with understanding and support.

For those who are mostly "trans," feeling that they are in the wrong body, various options apply, but given the dsyphoria and general emotional distress some degree of transitioning is often required. Hormonal treatments alone reduce the dsyphoria, because this intervention makes the person physically feel more like the gender they identify with. Feeling emotionally and physically like the sex other than their biological sex is often enough, and many individuals prefer to not have surgical reassignment. Complications from the surgery and unsatisfactory results, even in the most capable hands, can leave some of those who fully transition feeling just as bad, or even worse. Hence, it is important for those with a gender identity other than their biological sex not to assume they have to fully transition, and be open to a variety of options. Given that most instance of gender dysphoria and confusion during childhood resolve spontaneously, it is important to delay surgical interventions until it is clear that the transgender identity is permanent. It is also important to realize that if they retain their sexual organs and engage in sexual relations with those having the same organs, they are not "homosexual" but "heterosexual." Hence a male-to-female trans person without surgical reassignment who has sexual relationships with men is not "gay."

CORRECTING PERSPECTIVES:

In line with the concept of separate homoerotic and heteroerotic dimensions, the male-to-female trans person who has sexual relationships predominately with males, has a high heteroerotic motivation and a lower homoerotic motivation, as is usually the case with the men that engage in sexual relationships with them. This might

213

seem confusing and wrong to many still clinging to the notion that biological sex determines sexual orientation, but hopefully readers will appreciate from what has been presented that gender identity is the basis or anchor for sexual orientation. Readers will also appreciate that "homosexual" and "heterosexual" identities are a social construction, and the reality of human sexual orientation resides in separate homoerotic and heteroerotic dimensions that each of us have. Gender identity is the guide to and anchors what sex the homoerotic and heteroerotic dimensions apply to. A female gender identity means that the homoerotic dimension is active when the individual fantasizes about or engages with females, and the heterotic when such behavior involves males. A male gender identity means that the homoerotic dimension is active when the person fantasizes about or engages with men, and the heteroerotic when the focus is a female. By changing our perspectives in this fashion, transgender individuals can better accept themselves, and society at large understand them in an appropriate way fostering greater support and less discrimination, thereby making self-acceptance easier for transgender people.

CONCLUSION: THIS IS WHAT SEXUAL ORIENTATION IS ALL ABOUT!

It has been my goal to improve how we understand and conceptualize sexual orientation, such that we are more tolerant of variations from the norm in others and ourselves. In regards to others, there will then be less in the way of discrimination and persecution of homosexual, bisexual, and transgender individuals, and as pertains to the self, less guilt and greater self-acceptance. What might at first glance seem like an abstract academic notion, the evolutionary or Darwinian paradox turns out to be the key to an enlightened and comprehensive understanding of sexual orientation. Given that evolution and natural selection are facts of life, it has always been a dilemma how behavior not leading to reproduction could have evolved? Current psychological and biological theories fail to adequately explain this intriguing paradox, necessitating an entirely different perspective. Interestingly, researchers and theorists to date have tended to assume that homosexual and heterosexual identities are real entities. However, if they only approximate real occurrences then current theories will inevitably fall short of the mark. Our starting point in generating a more accurate understanding was animal homosexuality, clearly revealing how common homoerotic behavior is in the animal world, and not simply a fluke of human nature. Homoerotic behavior serves many purposes, in some instances ironically enhancing reproduction. In higher primates, certain functions are served by homoerotic behavior with clear implications for human sexuality—Tension reduction, reconciliation, and alliance formation, the latter being particularly applicable. Primates and humans appear to have relied on homoerotic behavior as a way of building alliances necessary for safety and survival, and also reproduction.

Beyond the functions served by homoerotic behavior, we explored the pivotal topic of whether sexual orientation is organized discretely or dimensionally. Our mind forces us to see things in discrete terms for purposes of simplification, while nature tends to be organized in a continuous fashion. Sexual orientation involves two separate dimensions, consisting of homoerotic and heteroerotic behavior, given the failure of a single dimension to capture the true nature of sexual orientation. These two dimensions equip us to function sexually in both same-sex and other-sex contexts, the former designed to reduce tensions, facilitate reconciliation, and promote alliance formation, amongst other functions. Heteroerotic behavior can serve these same functions in some instances, and of greatest significance is crucial for reproduction. This dual capacity has been an asset, and not a liability throughout our evolution. People vary in their level of homoerotic and heteroerotic motivation, and the dominant dimension is the one preferentially activated. However, given the right circumstances, the less dominant dimension can be activated, such as the need for same-sex alliance formation activating the homoerotic dimension. The concept of dimension activation and deactivation is a novel contribution to how we understand sexual orientation, and one that plays a key role in deciphering the impact of sexual abuse on subsequent sexual behavior.

Although no biological influence explains sexual orientation, genetics combined with events occurring during fetal development, probably provide each of us with a limited range of motivation on both the homoerotic and heteroerotic dimensions. As with personality dimensions, the value of a given level of motivation depends upon environmental circumstances, explaining why there is so much natural variation in homoerotic and heteroerotic motivation. In a setting where available mates are limited and competition fierce, a substantial motivation for same-sex alliance formation is advantageous, since a very high heteroerotic motivation might lead an individual to seek mates without proper alliance support, resulting in ostracism and perhaps even death. Conversely, in a setting where there are ample mates and limited competition, a higher heteroerotic and lower homoerotic motivation would be more adaptive. If an individual's given level of motivation on the homoerotic and heteroerotic dimensions align with environmental circumstances, he or she will be further ahead. Nature appears to have provided a non-zero motivation (at least when traumatic effects or mental illness are not an issue) on both dimensions, to facilitate homoerotic and heterorotic behavior when the need and opportunity arise, and of course the very presence of both dimensions provides us with some capacity.

The human mind is our greatest sex organ, and erotic fantasy plays a key role in sexual orientation by amplifying both homoerotic and heteroerotic motivations. This primarily takes the form of an entire level of sexuality beyond actual behavior. In non-human species sexuality probably consists just of behaviors, fantasy and imagination comprising a significant component only in humans. Erotic fantasy also plays a crucial role in activating sexual orientation dimensions, and can increase motivation for homoerotic and heteroerotic behavior over time. Behavior versus identity is the additional and final component that we require to understand sexual orientation. In animals, and apparently human societies prior to our modern industrial era, homoerotic and heteroerotic behaviors were all that counted. With industrialization we seem to have shifted to homo and hetero identities, forcing each of us to adopt one of these, or both (bisexuality). This social construction of human sexual orientation produces confusion, stress, anxiety, and frustration, given that nature has equipped us with both homoerotic and heteroerotic capacities and motivation. By shifting back to an emphasis on behaviors (including mental events), people will no longer have to identify with being homosexual, heterosexual, or bisexual, and be more accepting of both homoerotic and heteroerotic behavior. Far less negativity towards the self and others, based on sexual orientation, will follow from this enlightened shift from identity to behavior.

Transgender is much more easily understood when the concept of separate homoerotic and heteroerotic behavioral capacities is applied. Much as with homoerotic and heteroerotic behavior, masculinity and femininity occur on separate dimensions ensuring some mixture for each person. Sex hormones during fetal development, combined with genetic factors, influence the degree of masculine and feminine traits a person has, and hence their gender identity. Regardless of whether or not a person is "homosexual" or "heterosexual," gender identity tends to align with biological sex. However, due largely to alterations from the norm in sex hormone activity during fetal development misalignment does occur. Most transgender individuals end up with a fairly even mix of masculine and feminine traits, contributing to a dual (or neither) gender identity. In some instances though, a fully transgender scenario comes to pass, with feminine/masculine traits and gender identity other than biological sex. In such instances, and in contrast to much of the current thinking, "homosexual" and "heterosexual" designations must be based on and anchored by gender identity. Hence, a male-to-female transgender person attracted to males is "heterosexual." Applying the homoerotic and heteroerotic dimensions, such an individual has a high heteroerotic motivation and a low homoerotic motivation. By conceptually flipping or rotating our thinking transgender can be properly understood.

Considering our dual capacity for homoerotic and heteroerotic behavior, and also how we all have some mixing of masculine and feminine traits given the presence of separate dimensions in each of us, there is no need to use the socially constructed homosexual and heterosexual identity labels. Although not "real" entities these identities do describe relative homoerotic and heteroerotic motivations—"Homosexuality" being consistent with a high homoerotic motivation and low heteroerotic motivation, "heterosexuality" a high heteroerotic motivation and a low homoerotic motivation, bisexuality significant homoerotic and heteroerotic motivations, and asexuality very low or zero levels. Most people identify with being heterosexual due to the greater average heteroerotic motivation derived from the evolutionary fitness value of reproduction, and how homosexuality has a lesser social value based on it not being consistent with reproduction. Even then these labels represent an illusion, because we all appear to have some capacity and motivation to engage in both types of behavior, at least when free of guilt and inhibitions. This dual capacity resolves the evolutionary or Darwinian paradox, because homoerotic behavior does not preclude heteroerotic behavior, and in some instances even facilitates reproductive success. It is only when sexual orientation is based on homosexual and heterosexual identities, with the former excluding heteroerotic behavior that the evolutionary paradox arises. Dispensing with these erroneous identities and the whole emphasis on creating sexual identities, we can move forward and in the process return to a focus on behaviors. We will then be more accepting of homoerotic behavior and its expression alongside heteroerotic behavior. Resolving the conceptual evolutionary paradox has then provided us with a very practical way to understand and work with sexual orientation, and one that will foster greater social justice and self-acceptance.

Ω

REFERENCES

ABC News, (2012). Explorer27s-study-of-sexually-depraved-penguins-unearthed, June 12, http://www.abc.net.au/news/2012-06-10.

Adam, P.C., Murphy, D.A., & De Wit, J.B. (2011). When do online sexual fantasies become reality? The contribution of erotic chatting via the internet to sexual risk-taking in gay and other men who have sex with men. Health Education Research, 26(3), 506-515.

Adriaens, P.R., De Block, A. (2006). The evolution of social construction: The case of male homosexuality. Perspectives In Biological And Medicine, 49(4), 570-585.

Akers, J., & Conway, C. (1979). Female homosexual behavior. Macaca mulatta. Archives of Sexual Behavior, 8, 63-80.

Allen, L.S., & Gorski, R.A. (1992). Sexual orientation and the size of the anterior commissure in the human brain. Proceedings Of The National Academy Of Science USA, 89(15), 7199-7202.

Asthana, S., & Oostvogels, R. (2001). The social construction of male 'homosexuality' in India: Implications for HIV transmission and prevention. Social Science And Medicine, 52(5), 707-721.

Bagemihl, B. (1999). Biological Exuberance: Animal Homosexuality And Natural Diversity. New York: St. Martin's Press.

Bailey, J.M., Dunne, M.P., & Martin, N.G. (2000). Genetic and environmental influences on sexual orientation and its correlates in an Australian twin sample. Journal Of Personality And Social Psychology, 78(3), 524-536.

Bailey, J.M., & Pillard, R.C. (1991). A genetic study of male sexual orientation. Archives of General Psychiatry, 48, 1089-1094.

Bailey, J.M., Pillard, R.C., Neale, M.C., & Agyei, Y. (1993). Heritable factors influence sexual orientation in women. Archives Of General Psychiatry, 50(3), 217-223.

Bailey, J.M., & Zucker, K.J. (1995). Childhood sex-typed behavior and sexual orientation: A conceptual analysis and quantitative review. Developmental Psychology, 31, 43-55.

Barish DP. Sociobiology And Behavior. New York: Elsevier 1982.

Baron, M. (1993). Genetic linkage and male homosexual orientation. BMJ, 307, 338-347.

Bearman, P.S., & Bruckner, H. (2002). Opposite-sex twins and adolescent same-sex attraction. American Journal of Sociology, 107(5), 1179-1205.

Behrman, K.D., & Kirpatrick, M. (2011). Species range expansion by beneficial mutations. Journal Of Evolutionary Biology, 24(3), 665-675.

Bell, A.P., Weinberg, M.S., & Hammersmith, S.K. (1981). Sexual Preference: Its Development In Men And Women. Bloomington: Indiana University.

Bem, S.L. (1975). Sex-role adaptability: One consequence of psychological androgyny. Journal Of Personality And Social Psychology, 31, 634-643.

Bem, D.J. (1996). Exotic becomes erotic: A developmental theory of sexual orientation. Psychological Review, 103(2), 320-335.

Bemporad, J.R. (1991). Dementia praecox as a failure of neoteny. Theoretical Medicine, 12, 45-51.

Bentz, E., Hefler, L., Kaufmann, U., Huber, J., Kolbus, A., & Tempfer, C. (2008). A polymorphism of the CYP17 gene related to sex steroid metabolism is associated with female-to-male but not male-to-female transsexualism. Fertility And Sterility, 90(1), 56-59.

Berger, P., & Luckman, T. (1991). The Social Construction Of Reality. London: Penguin Books.

Bhugra, D., McMullen, I., & Popelyuk, D. (2010). Paraphilias across cultures: Contexts and controversies. The Journal of Sex Research, 47(2-3), 242-262.

Bhugra, D., Rahman, Q., & Bhintade, R. (2006). Sexual fantasy in gay men in India: A comparison with heterosexual men. Sexual And Relationship Therapy, 21(2), 197-207.

Bieber, I., Dain, H.J., Dince, P.R., Drelich, M.C., Grand, H.G., Gundlach, R.H., et al. (1962). Homosexuality: A Psychoanalytic Study Of Male Homosexuals. New York: Basic Books.

Blackwood, E. (1985). Breaking the mirror: The construction of lesbianism and the anthropological discourse on homosexuality. Journal Of Homosexuality, 11(3-4), 1-17.

Blanchard, R. (1985). Typology of male-to-female transsexualism. Archives Of Sexual Behavior, 14(3), 247-261.

Blanchard, R. (1989). The classification and labeling of nonhomosexual gender dysphorias. Archives Of Sexual Behavior, 18, 315-334.

Blanchard, R. (1991). Clinical observations and systematic studies of autogynephilia. Journal Of Sex & Marital Therapy, 17(4), 235-251.

Blanchard, R. (2008). Review and theory of handedness, birth order, and homosexuality in men. Laterality, 2008, 13(1), 51-70.

Boelkins, R.C., & Wilson, R.P. (1972). Intergroup social dynamics of the Cayo Santiago rhesus (macaca mulatta) with special reference to changes in group membership by males. Primates, 13, 125-140.

Bowins, B.E. (2004). Psychological defense mechanisms: A new perspective. American Journal of Psychoanalysis, 64, 1-26.

Bowins, B.E. (2014). At The Tipping Point: How To Save Us From Self-Destruction, Infinity Publishing, 2014.

Boswell, J. (1980). Christianity, Social Tolerance, And Homosexuality. Chicago: University of Chicago Press.

Boswell, J. (1994). Same-Sex Unions In Premodern Europe. New York: Villard Books.

Boucher, J., & Carlson, G. (1980). Recognition of facial expression in three cultures. Journal Of Cross-Cultural Psychology, 11, 263-280.

Braithwaite, L.W. (1970). The black swan. Australian Natural History, 16, 375-379.

Bramblett, J.R., & Darling, C.A. (1997). Sexual contacts: Experiences, thoughts, and fantasies of adult male survivors of child sexual abuse. Journal of Sex & Marital Therapy, 23(4), 313, 23-36.

Braaten, L.J., & Darling C.D. (1965). Overt and covert homosexual problems among male college students. Genetic Psychology Monographs, 71, 302-303.

Brewer, M., & Miller, N. (1996). Intergroup Relations. Buckingham, England: Open University Press.

Briley, D.A., & Tucker-Drob, E.M. (2012). Broad bandwidth or high fidelity? Evidence from the structure of genetic and environmental effects on the facets of the five factor model. Behavioral Genetics, 42(5), 743-763.

Brousseau, L., Bonal, D., Cigna, J., & Scotti, I. (2013). Highly local environmental variability promotes intrapopulation divergence of quantitative traits: An example from tropical rain forest trees. Annals Of Botany, 112(6), 1169-1179.

224

Brown, D.G. (1963). Homosexuality and family dynamics. Bulletin of the Menninger Clinic, 27(5), 28-43.

Burton, S. (2006). The Causes Of Homosexuality: What Science Tells Us. Cambridge: The Jubilee Centre.

Byne, W. (1995). Science and belief: Psychobiological research on sexual orientation. Journal Of Homosexuality, 28(3-4), 303-344.

Byne, W., & Parsons, B. (1993). Human sexual orientation. The biological theories reappraised. Archives Of General Psychiatry, 50(3), 228-239.

Byne, W., Tobet, S., & Mattiace, L.A. (2001). The interstitial nuclei of the anterior hypothalamus: An investigation of variance with sex, sexual orientation, and HIV status. Hormones and Behavior, 40(2), 86-92.

Cado, S., & Leitenberg, H. (1990). Guilt reactions to sexual fantasies during intercourse. Archives Of Sexual Behavior, 19, 49-63.

Calam, R., Horne, L., Glasgow, D., & Cox, A. (1998). Psychological disturbance and child sexual abuse: A follow-up study. Child Abuse & Neglect, 22(9), 901-913.

Calleja-Agius, J., Mallia, P., Sapiano, K., & Schembri-Wismayer, P. (2012). A review of the management of intersex. Neonatal Network, 31(2), 97103.

Cameron, P. (1967). Note on time spent thinking about sex. Psychological Reports, 20, 741-742.

Canadian Psychological Association. (2013). "Psychology works" fact sheet: Gender dysphoria in children. Canadian Psychological Association Fact Sheet, Page 1-4.

Cantarella, E. (1992). Bisexuality In The Ancient World. New Haven: Yale University Press.

Cantor, J.M., Blanchard, R., Paterson, A.D., & Bogaert, A.F. (2002). How many gay men owe their sexual orientation to fraternal birth order? Archives of Sexual Behavior, 31(1), 63-71.

Carey, B. (2005). Straight, gay, or lying?: Bisexuality revisited. The New York Times, July 5.

Carvalho, J., Gomes, A.Q., Laja, P., Oliveira, C., Vilarinho, S., Janssen, E., & Nobre, P. (2013). Gender differences in sexual arousal and affective responses to erotica: The effects of type of film and fantasy instruction. Archives Of Sexual Behavior, 42(6), 1011-1019.

Catalyst Knowledge Center. (2012). Catalyst Quick Take: Lesbian, Gay, Bisexual & Transgender Workplace Issues. New York: Catalyst.

Chevin, L.M., & Lande, R. Evolution of discrete phenotypes from continuous norms of reaction. American Naturalist, 182(1), 13-27.

Chung, W.C., De Vries, G.J., & Swaab, D.F. (2002). Sexual differentiation of the bed nucleus of the stria terminalis in humans may extend into adulthood. The Journal Of Neuroscience, 22(3), 1027-1033.

Ciani, A.C., Cermelli, P., & Zanzotto, G. (2008). Sexually antagonistic selection in human male homosexuality. Plos One, 3(6), e2282.

Coleman, E, Gooren, L., & Ross, M. (1989). Theories of gender transpositions: A critique and suggestions for further research. The Journal of Sex Research, 26(4), 525-538.

Columbia News Service (2002). They're in love. They're gay. They're penguins. Columbia University, Columbia News Service, http://timelessspirit.com/Sept04/cristina.shtml

Conway, L. (2002). What causes transsexualism? http://al/eecs.umich.edu/people/conway/TS/TScauses.html

Costa, P.T., & McCrae, R.R. (1992). Revised NEO Personality (NEO-PI-R) And NEO Fve Factor Inventory (NEO-FFI)

Professional Journal Manual. Odessa Florida: Psychological Assessment Resources.

Crepault, C., & Coulture, M. (1980). Men's erotic fantasies. Archives Of Sexual Behavior, 9(6), 565-581.

Critelli, J.W., & Bivona, J.M. (2008). Women's erotic rape fantasies: An evaluation of theory and research. Journal Of Sex Research, 45(1), 57-70.

Crompton. L. (2003). Homosexuality And Civilization. Cambridge: Harvard University Press.

Darwin, C. (1858). On The Origin Of Species. New York, Signet Classic, 1858/1958.

Davies, N.B. (1991). Mating systems. In J.R. Krebs and N.B. Davies (Eds.), Behavioural Ecology: An Evolutionary Approach (Third Edition) (pp. 263-294). Boston: Blackwell Scientific Publications.

Denniston, R.H. (1980). Ambisexuality in animals. In J. Marmor (Ed.), Homosexual Behavior: A Modern Reappraisal (pp. 25-40). New York: Basic Books.

De Rooij, S.R., Veenendaal, M.V., Raikkonen, K., & Roseboom, T.J. (2012). Personality and stress appraisal in adults prenatally exposed to the Dutch famine. Early Human Development, 88(5), 321-325.

deWaal, F. (1982). Chimpanzee Politics: Power And Sex Among Apes. New York: Harper & Row.

deWaal, F., & Lansing, F. (1997). Bonobo: The Forgotten Ape. Berkeley: University of California Press.

Diamond, L.M. (2006). The evolution of plasticity in female-female desire. Journal of Psychology & Human Sexuality, 18(4), 245-274.

Dickemann, M. (1993). Reproductive strategies and gender construction: An evolutionary view of homosexualities. Journal Of Homosexuality, 24(3-4), 55-71.

Dickemann, M. (1995). Wilson panchreston: The inclusive fitness hypothesis of sociobiology re-examined. Journal Of Homosexuality, 28(1-2), 147-183.

Dorner, G. (1980). Sexual differentiation of the brain. Vitamins And Minerals, 38, 325-381.

Dover, K.J. (1989). Greek Homosexuality. Cambridge: Harvard University Press.

Dunbar, E. (2006). Race, gender, and sexual orientation in hate crime victimization: Identity politics or identity risk? Violence And Victims, 21(3), 323-327.

Dunkle, S.W. (1991). Head damage from mating attempts in dragonflies. Entomological News, 102(1), 37-41.

Easpaig, B.R., Fryer, D.M., Linn, S.E., & Humphrey, R.H. (2014). A queer-theoretical approach to community health psychology. Journal Of Health Psychology, 19(1), 117-125.

Edwards, A.A., & Todd, J.D. (1991). Homosexual behaviour in wild white-handed gibbons (hylobates lar). Primates, 32(2), 231-236.

Ekman, P., & Friesen, W. (1971). Constants across cultures in the face and emotion. Journal Of Personality And Social Psychology, 17, 124-129.

Ellis, B.J., & Simmons, D. (1990). Sex differences in sexual fantasy: An evolutionary approach. Journal Of Sex Research, 27, 527-555.

Eschoffier, J. (1998). American Homo: Community And Perversity. Berkely: University Of California Press.

Estes, L.S., & Tidwell, R. (2002). Sexually abused children's behaviors: Impact of gender and mother's experience of intra- and extra-familial sexual abuse. Family Practice, 19(1), 36-44.

European Union Agency For Fundamental Rights. (2012). European union lesbian, gay, bisexual, and transgender survey.

Evans, R.B. (1969). Childhood parental relationships of homosexual men. Journal Of Counseling And Clinical Psychology, 33, 129-133.

Fahs, B. (2009). Compulsory bisexuality?: The challenges of modern sexual fluidity. Journal Of Bisexuality, 9, 431-449.

Fairbanks, L.A., McGuire, M.T., & Kerber, W. (1977). Sex and aggression during rhesus monkey group formation. Aggression and Behavior, 3, 241-249.

Farr, D., & Degroult, N. (2008). Understand the queer world of the L-esbian body: Using queer as folk and the l word to address the construction of the lesbian body. Journal Of Lesbian Studies, 12(4), 423-434.

Fitzgerald, T.K. (1977). A critique of anthropological research on homosexuality. Journal Of Homosexuality, 2(4), 385-397.

Focault, M. (1980). The History Of Sexuality. New York: Vintage Books.

Ford, C.S., & Beach, F.A. (1951). Patterns Of Sexual Behavior. New York: Harper.

Fox, E.A. (2001). Homosexual behavior in wild Sumatran orangutans (pongo pygmaeus abelii). American Journal Of Primatology, 55(3), 177-181.

Freud, S. (1905/1962). Three Essays On The Theory Of Sexuality, trans. James Strachey. New York: Basic Books.

Freud, S. (1908/1962). Creative writers and daydreaming. In J. Strachy (Ed.). The Standard Edition Of The Complete Psychological Works Of Sigmund Freud (Vol. 9, pp. 142-152). London: Hogarth.

Freund, K., Steiner, B.W., & Chan, S. (1982). Two types of cross-gender identity. Archives Of Sexual Behavior, 11, 49-63.

Gammon, M.A., & Isgro, K.L. (2006). Troubling the canon: Bisexuality and queer theory. Journal Of Homosexuality, 52(1-2), 159-184.

Garcia-Falgueras, A., & Swaab, D.F. (2008). A sex difference in the hypothalamic uncinate nucleus: Relationship to gender identity. Brain, 131(12), 3132-3146.

Glantz,, K. & Pearce, J. (1989). Exiles From Eden: Psychotherapy From An Evolutionary Perspective. New York: W.W. Norton & Company.

Gold, S.R., & Gold, R.G. (1991). Gender differences in first sexual fantasies. Journal Of Sex Education And Therapy, 17, 207-216.

Goodall, J. (1965). Chimpanzees of the gombe stream reserve. In I. DeVore (Ed.), Primate Behavior: Field Studies Of Monkeys And Apes (pp. 425-473). New York: Holt, Rinehart, & Winston.

Gooren, L.J., & Kruijver, F.P. (2002). Androgens and male behavior. Molecular & Cellular Endocrinology, 198(1-2), 31-40

Greenfield, M., Mazur, T., Michal, G., & Quattrin, T. (2010). Management of children with ambiguous genitalia using a "disorders of sex development (DSD) team." Journal Of Urology, 182(Suppl 4), pp e209.

Hall, D.K., Mathews, F., & Pearce, J. (1998). Factors associated with sexual behavior in young sexually abused children. Child Abuse & Neglect, 22(10), 1045-1063.

Hamer, D.H., Hu, S., Magnuson, V.L., Hu, N., & Pattatucci, A.M. (1993). A linkage between DNA markers on the x-chromosome and male sexual orientation. Science, 261, 321-327.

Hanby, J.P., Robertson, L.T., & Phoenix, C.H. (1971). The sexual behavior of a confined troop of Japanese macaques. Folia Primatologica, 16, 123-143.

Hare, L., Bernard, P., Sanchez, F., Baird, P., Vilain, E., Kennedy, T., & Harley, V. (2009). Androgen receptor repeat length polymorphism associated with male-to-female transsexualism. Biological Psychiatry, 65(1), 93-96.

Harrison, M.A., Hughes, S.M., Burch, R.L., & Gallup, G.G. (2008). The impact of prior heterosexual experiences on homosexuality in women. Evolutionary Psychology, 6(2), 316-327.

Haumann, G. (1995). Homosexuality, biology, and ideology. Journal Of Homosexuality, 28(1-2), 57-77.

Heenen-Wolff, S. (2011). Infantile bisexuality and the 'complete oedipal complex': Freudian views on heterosexuality and homosexuality. International Journal Of Psychoanalysis, 92(5), 1209-1220.

Herdt, G.H. (1988). Cross-cultural forms of homosexuality and the concept 'gay.' Psychiatric Annals, 18(1), 37-39.

Herdt, G. (1998). Same Sex, Different Cultures. New York: West View Press.

Herzing, D.L., & Johnson, C.M. (1997). Interspecific interactions between spotted dolphins (stenella frontalis) and bottlenose dolphins (tursiops truncatus) in the Bahamas, 1985-1995. Aquatic Mammals, 23, 85-99.

Hines, M. (2006). Prenatal testosterone and gender-related behaviour. European Journal Of Endocrinology, 155(Suppl 1), 115-121.

Hinsch, B. (1990). Passions Of The Cut Sleeve: The Male Homosexual Tradition In China. Berkeley: University of California Press.

Ho, P.S. (1995). Male homosexual identity in Hong Kong: A social construction. Journal Of Homosexuality, 29(1), 71-88.

Hotte, J.P., & Rafman, S. (1992). The specific effects of incest on prepubertal girls from dysfunctional families. Child Abuse & Neglect, 16(2), 273-283.

Hu, S., Wei, N., Wang, Q.D., Yan, L.Q., Wei, E.Q., Zhang, M.M., et al. (2008). Patterns of brain activation during visually evoked sexual arousal differ between homosexual and heterosexual men. AJNR American Journal Of Neuroradiology, 29(10), 1890-1896.

Hutchinson, G.E. (1959). A speculative consideration of certain forms of sexual selection in men. American Nature, 93, 81-91.

Iasenza, S. (2010). What is queer about sex? Expanding sexual frames in theory and practice. Family Processes, 49(3), 291-308.

Ioannidis, J. (2005). Why most published research findings are false. PLoS Med, 2(8): e24.

James, W.H. (2005). Biological and psychosocial determinants of male and female sexual orientation. Journal Of Biosocial Science, 37(5), 555-567.

Kangassalo, K., Polkki, M., & Rantala, M.J. (2011). Prenatal influences on sexual orientation: Digit ratio (2D:4D) and the number of older siblings. Evolutionary Psychology, 9(4), 496-508.

Kano, T. (1992). The Last Ape: Pygmy Chimpanzee Behavior And Ecology. Standford, CA: Stanford University Press.

Kauth, M. (2000). True Nature: A Theory Of Sexual Attraction. New York: Springer.

Kennedy, M. (2010). Rural men, sexual identity and community. Journal Of Homosexuality, 57(8), 1051-1091.

Kinsey, A.C., Pomeroy, W.B., & Martin, C.E. (1948). Sexual Behavior In The Human Male. Philadelphia: W.B. Saunders.

Kinsey, A.C., Pomeroy, W.B., Martin, C.E., & Gebhard, P.H. (1953). Sexual Behavior In The Human Female. Philadelphia: W.B. Saunders.

Kirsch, J.A., & Rodman, J.E. (1982). Selection and sexuality: The Darwinian view of homosexuality. In W. Paul & J.D. Weinrich (Eds.), Homosexuality: Social, Psychological, And Biological Issues (pp. 183-195). Beverly Hills: Sage Publications.

Klein, F. (1993). The Bisexual Option. New York: Haworth Press.

Klein, F., Sepekoff, B., & Wolf, T.J. (1985). Sexual orientation: A multi-variable dynamic process. Journal Of Homosexuality, 11, 35-49.

Knauft, B.M. (2003). What ever happened to ritualized homosexuality? Modern sexual subjects in Melanesia and elsewhere, 14, 137-159.

Kruijver, F.P., Zhou, J.N., Pool, C.W., Hofman, M.A., Gooren, L.J., & Swaab, D.F. (2000). Male-to-female transsexuals have female neuron numbers in a limbic nucleus. Journal Of Endocrinology & Metabolism, 85(5), 2034-2041.

Larson, P.C. (1981). Sexual identity and self-concept. Journal of Homosexuality, 7(1), 15-32.

Lasco, M.S., Jordan, T.J., Edgar, M.A., Petito, C.K., & Byne, W. (2002). A lack of dimorphism of sex or sexual orientation in the human anterior commissure. Brain Research, 936, 95-105.

Lehne, G.K. (1978). Gay male fantasies and realities. Journal Of Social Issues, 34, 28-37.

Leitenberg, H., & Henning, K. (1995). Sexual fantasy. Psychological Bulletin, 117(3), 469-496.

Lentz, S.L., & Zeiss, A.M. (1983). Fantasy and sexual arousal in college women: An empirical investigation. Imagination, Cognition, And Personality, 3, 185-202.

Levan, K.E., Fedina, T.Y., & Lewis, S.M. (2009). Testing multiple hypotheses for the maintenance of male homosexual copulatory behavior in flour beetles. Journal Of Evolutionary Biology, 22(1), 60-70.

LeVay, S. (1991). A difference in hypothalamic structure between heterosexual and homosexual men. Science, 253(30), 1034-1037.

LeVay (2012). Gay, Straight, And The Reason Why: The Science Of Sexual Orientation. New York: Oxford University Press.

Lippa, R.A. (2005). Sexual orientation and personality. Annual Review Of Sex Research, 16, 119-153.

Lyons, C. (2006). Stigma or sympathy? Attributions of fault to hate crime victims and offenders. Social Psychology Quarterly, 69(1), 39-59.

MacIntyre, F., & Estep, K.W. (1993). Sperm competition and the persistence of genes for male homosexuality. Biosystems, 31, 223-233.

Mackey, W.C. (1990). Adult-male/juvenile association as a species-characteristic human trait: A comparative field approach. In J.R. Feierman (Ed), Pedophilia: Biosocial Dimensions (pp. 299-323). New York: Springer-Verlag.

MacLusky, N.J., & Naftolin, F. (1981). Sexual differentiation of the central nervous system. Science, 211, 1294-1303.

Maeve, M.K. (1999). The social construction of love and sexuality in a women's prison. ANS Advanced Nursing Science, 21(3), 46-65.

McKenzie, S. (2010). Genders and sexualities in individuation: Theoretical and clinical explorations. Journal Of Analytical Psychology, 55(1), 91-111.

McLaughlin, K.A., Hatzenbuehler, M.L., Xuan, Z., & Conron, K.J. (2012). Disproportionate exposure to early-life adversity and sexual orientation disparities in psychiatric morbidity. Child Abuse & Neglect, 36(9), 645-655.

McRuer, R. (1993). A visitation of difference: Randall Kenan and black queer theory. Journal Of Homosexuality, 26(2-3), 221-232.

Mahurin, R.K., Velligan, D.I., & Miller, A.L. (1998). Executive-frontal lobe cognitive dysfunction in schizophrenia: A symptom subtype analysis. Psychiatry Research, 79, 139-149.

Mehlman, P.T., & Chapais, B. (1988). Differential effects of kinship, dominance, and the mating season on female allogrooming in a captive group of macaca fuscata. Primates, 29(2), 195-217.

Meyer-Bahlburg, H.F. (1982). Hormones and psychosexual differentiation: Implications for the management of intersexuality, homosexuality, and transsexuality. Clinics in Endocrinology and Metabolism, 11(3), 681-701.

Middleton, W. (2013). Ongoing incestuous abuse during adulthood. Journal Of Trauma & Dissociation, 14(3), 251-272.

Miller, E.M. (2000). Homosexuality, birth order, and evolution: Toward an equilibrium reproductive economics of homosexuality. Archives Of Sexual Behavior, 29(1), 1-34.

Mitchell, G. (1979). Behavioral Sex Differences In Nonhuman Primates. New York: Van Nostrand Reinhold Company.

Money, J. (1988). Gay, Straight, And In-Between: The Sexology Of Erotic Orientation. New York: Oxford University Press.

Mori, U. (1979). Development of sociability and social status. In M. Kawai (Ed.), Ecological And Sociological Studies Of Gelada Baboons (pp. 125-154). Tokyo: Kodansha-Karger.

Moser, C. (2010). Blanchard's autogynephilia theory: A critique. Journal Of Homosexuality, 57(6), 790-809.

Murray, J.B. (2000). Psychological profile of pedophiles and child molesters. The Journal of Psychology, 134(2), 211-224.

Muscarella, F. (1999). The homoerotic behavior that never evolved. Journal of Homosexuality, 37(3), 1-18.

Muscarella, F. (2000). The evolution of homoerotic behavior in humans. Journal of Homosexuality, 40(1), 51-77.

Mustanski, B.S., Dupree, M.G., Niervergelt, C.M., Bocklandt, S., Schork, N.J., & Hamer, D.H. (2005). A genomewide scan of male sexual orientation. Human Genetics, 116(4), 272-278.

Noel, J., Wann, D., & Branscombe, N. (1995). Peripheral ingroup membership status and public negativity towards outgroups. Journal Of Personality And Social Psychology, 68(1), 127-137.

Norris, K.S., & Dohl, T.P. (1980). Behaviour of the Hawaiin spinner dolphin, stenella longirostris. Fishery Bulletin, 77, 821-849.

O'Connor, P.J. (1964). Aetiological factors in homosexuality as seen in Royal Air Force psychiatric practice. British Journal Of Psychiatry, 110, 384-385.

Paoli, T., Palagi, E., Tacconi, G., & Tarli, S.B. (2006). Perineural swelling, intermenstrual cycle, and female sexual behavior in bonobos (pan paniscus). American Journal Of Primatology, 68(4), 333-347.

Parish, A.R. (1994). Sex and food control in the "uncommon chimpanzee": How bonobo females overcome a phylogenetic legacy of male dominance. Ethology And Sociobiology, 15, 157-194.

Paul, T., Schiffer, B., Zwarg, T., Kruger, T.H., Karama, S., Schedlowski, N., et al. (2008). Brain response to visual sexual stimuli in heterosexual and homosexual males. Human Brain Mapping, 29(6), 726-735.

236

Pedersen, W., & Kristiansen, H.W. (2008). Homosexual experience, desire and identity among young adults. Journal Of Homosexuality, 54(1-2), 68-102.

Pelletier, L.A., & Herold, E.S. (1988). The relationship of age, sex guilt, and sexual experience with female sexual fantasies. Journal Of Sex Research, 24(1), 250-256.

PFLAG Canada. (2006). Support For Transgender Individuals. www.pflagcanada.ca

Plato. (1981). The Symposium. Translated by Trevor Saunders. New York: Bantam Books.

Poiani, A. (2010). Animal Homosexuality: A Biosocial Approach. Cambridge: Cambridge University Press.

Price, J.H., Allensworth, D.D., Hill, K.S. (1985). Comparison of sexual fantasies of homosexuals and heterosexuals. Psychological Reports, 57, 871-877.

Priebe, G., & Svedin, C.G. (2013). Operationalization of three dimensions of sexual orientation in a national survey of late adolescents. Journal Of Sexual Research, 50(8), 727-738.

Prince, J.H., Allensworth, D.D., & Hillman, K. (1985). Comparison of sexual fantasies of homosexuals and heterosexuals. Psychological Reports, 57, 871-877.

Psych Central. (2013). Gender dysphoria symptoms. American Psychiatry Association, December 13, http://psychcentral.com/disorders/gender-dysphoria

Pusey, A.E., & Packer, C. (1987). Dispersal and philopatry. In B.B Smuts, D.L. Cheney, R.M. Seyfarth, R.W. Wrangham, & T.T. Struhsaker (Eds.), Primate Societies (pp. 250-266). Chicago: Chicago University Press.

Putnam, F.W. (2003). Ten-year research update review: Child sexual abuse. Journal Of The American Academy Of Child And Adolescent Psychiatry, 42(3), 269-278.

Rahman, Q. (2005). The neurodevelopment of sexual orientation. Neuroscience And Biobehavioral Reviews, 29(7), 1057-1066.

Reiss, D. (2011). The Dolphin In The Mirrror. Boston: Houghton Mifflin Harcourt.

Reynolds, K., Turner, J., & Haslam, S. (2000). When are we better than them and they worse than us? A closer look at social discrimination in positive and negative domains. Journal Of Personality And Social Psychology, 78(1), 64-80.

Rice, G., Anderson, C., Risch, N., & Ebers, G. (1999). Male homosexuality: Absence of linkage to microsatellite markers at xq28. Science, 284, 666-678.

Richters, J., De Visser, R.O., Rissel, C.E., Grulich, A.E., & Smith, A. (2008). Demographics and psychosocial features of participants in bondage and discipline, "sadomasochism" or dominance and submission (BDSM): Data from a national survey. The Journal Of Sexual Medicine, 5(7), 1660-1668.

Robinson, C. (2006). Developing an identity model for transgender and intersex inclusion in lesbian communities. Journal Of Lesbian Studies, 10(1-2), 181-199.

Rodriguez, T. (2013). Life satisfaction linked to personality changes. Scientific American Mind, July/August, 8-9.

Roselli, C.E., & Stormshak, F. (2009). Prenatal programming of sexual partner preference: The ram model. Journal Of Neuroendocrinology, 21(4), 359-364.

Ross, A. (1973). Celtic and northern art. In P. Rawson (Ed.), Primitive Erotic Art (pp. 77-106). New York: G.P. Putman & Sons.

Saewyc, E.M., Carol, L., Skay, S.L., Pettingell, E.A., Reis, L.B., Resnick, M. et al (2006). Hazards of stigma: The sexual and physical abuse of gay, lesbian, and bisexual adolescents in the United States and Canada. Child Welfare, 85(2), 195-213.

Sala, A., & De la Mata Benitez, M.L. (2009). Devloping lesbian identity: A sociohistorical approach. Journal Of Homosexuality, 56(7), 819-838.

Sampaio, A., Soares, J.M., Coutinho, J., Sousa, N., & Goncalves, O.F. (2013). The big five default brain: Functional evidence. Brain Structure And Function, 24, 51-62.

Savage-Rumbaugh, E.S., & Wilkerson, B.J. (1978). Socio-sexual behavior in pan paniscus and pan troglodytes: A comparative study. Journal of Human Evolution, 7, 327-344.

Serano, J.M. (2010). The case against autogynephilia. International Journal Of Transgenderism, 12(3), 176-187.

Sherif, M. (1961). Intergroup Conflict And Cooperation: The Robbers Cave Experiment. Norman, Oklahoma: University Of Oklahoma Book Exchange.

Shively, M.G., & De Cecco, J.P. (1977). Components of sexual identity. Journal of Homosexuality, 3(1), 41-48.

Shorter, E. (1997). A History Of Psychiatry. Toronto: John Wiley & Sons, Inc

Singer, B. (1985). A comparison of evolutionary and environmental theories of erotic response: Part II. Empirical arenas. Journal Of Sex Research, 21, 345-374.

Sismondo, S. (1993). Some social constructions. Social Studies Of Science, 23, 515-553.

Small, M.F. (1993). Female Choices: Sexual Behavior Of Female Primates. Ithaca, NY: Cornell University Press.

Small, M.F. (1995). What's Love Got To Do With It? The Evolution Of Human Mating. New York: Doubleday.

Smith, D., & Over, R. (1990). Enhancement of fantasy-induced sexual arousal in men through training in sexual imagery. Archives Of Sexual Behavior, 19(5), 477-489.

Smuts, B.B., & Watanabe, J.M. (1990). Social relationships and ritualized greetings in adult male baboons (papio cynocephalus Anubis). International Journal of Primatology, 11, 147-172.

Stanford Encyclopedia Of Philosophy. (2011). Homosexuality. http://plato.stanford.edu/entries/homosexuality/

Stevens, P.E., & Hall, J.M. (1991). A critical historical analysis of the medical construction of lesbianism. International Journal Of Health Services, 21(2), 291-307.

Stoleru, S., Gregire, M.C., & Gerald, D. (1999). Neuroanatomical correlates of visually evoked sexual arousal in human males. Archives Of Sexual Behavior, 28, 1-21.

Stoller, R.J., & Herdt, G.H. (1985). Theories of origins of male homosexuality. Archives of General Psychiatry, 42, 399-404.

Storms, M.D. (1980). Theories of sexual orientation. Journal of Personality & Social Psychology, 38(5), 783-792.

Sugiyama, Y. (1969). Social behavior of chimpanzees in the budongo forest, Uganda. Primates, 10, 197-225.

Swaab, D.F. (2004). Sexual differentiation of the human brain: Relevance for gender identity, transsexualism and sexual orientation. Gynecological Endocrinology, 19(6), 301-312.

Swaab, D.F., & Fliess, E. (1985). A sexual dimorphic nucleus in the human brain. Science, 228, 1112-1114.

Swaab, D.F., & Hofman, M.A. (1990). An enlarged suprachiasmatic nucleus in homosexual men. Brain Research, 537(1-2), 141-148.

Taub, D.M. (1990). The functions of primate paternalism: A cross-species review. In J.R. Feierman (Ed.), Pedophilia: Biosocial Dimensions (pp. 338-377). New York: Springer-Verlag.

Thorp, J. (1992). Review article/discussion: The social construction of homosexuality. Phoenix, 46(1), 54-65.

Tither, J.M., & Ellis, B.J. (2008). Impact of fathers on daughters' age at menarche: A genetically and environmentally controlled sibling study. Developmental Psychology, 44(5), 1409-1420.

Torgersen, A.M., & Janson, H. (2002). Why do identical twins differ in personality: Shared environment reconsidered. Twin Research, 5(1), 44-52.

Transgender London. (2013). Not a choice? What causes it? www.transgenderlondon.com/What%20Causes%20It.htm

Valenzuela, C.Y. (2010). Sexual orientation, handedness, sex ratio and fetomaternal tolerance-rejection. Biological Research, 43(3), 347-356.

Van der Dennen, J.M. (1995). The Origins Of War: The Evolution Of Male-Coalitional Reproductive Strategy. Groningen, Netherlands: Origin Press.

Vanderlaan, D.P., Blanchard, R., Wood, H., & Zucker, K.J. (2014). Birth order and sibling sex ratio of children and adolescents referred to a gender identity service. Plos One, 9(3), e90257.

Vanderlaan, D.P., Forrester, D.L., Petterson, L.J., & Vasey, P.L. (2012). Offspring production among the extended relatives of Samoan men and fa'afafine. Plos One, 7(4), e36088.

Vanderlaan, D.P., & Vasey, P.L. (2011). Male sexual orientation in independent Samoa: Evidence for fraternal birth order and maternal fecundity effects. Archives of Sexual Behavior, 40(3), 495-503.

Vasey, P.L. (1995). Homosexual behavior in primates: A review of evidence and theory. International Journal of Primatology, 16(2), 173-203.

Vasey, P.L. (2004). Sex differences in sexual partner acquisition, retention, and harassment during female homosexual consortships in Japanese macaques. American Journal Of Primatology, 64(4), 397-409.

Vasey, P.L., & Jiskoot, H. (2010). The biogeography and evolution of female homosexual behavior in Japanese macaques. Archives Of Sexual Behavior, 39(6), 1439-1441.

Walen, S.R., & Roth, D. (1987). A cognitive approach. In J.H. Geer & W.T. O'Donohue (Eds), Theories Of Human Sexuality (pp.335-362). New York: Plenum Press.

Weeks, J. (1985). Sexuality And Its Discontents. London: Routledge And Kegan Paul.

Weinrich, J.D. (1980). Homosexual behavior in animals: A new review of observations from the wild and their relationship to human sexuality. In R. Forleo, & W. Pasini (Eds.), Medical Sexology: The Third International Congress (pp. 288-295). Littleton, MA: PSG Publishing.

Weinrich, J.D. (1982). Is homosexuality biologically natural? In W. Paul & J.D. Weinrich (Eds.), Homosexuality: Social, Psychological, And Biological Issues (pp. 197-208). Beverly Hills: Sage Publications.

Weinrich, J.D., Snyder, P.J., Pillard, R.C., Grant, I., Jacobson, D.L., Robinson, S.R., & McCutchan, J.A. (1993). A factor analysis of the Klein Sexual Orientation Grid in two disparate samples. Archives Of Sexual Behavior, 22, 157-168.

West, D.J. (1977). Homosexuality Re-Examined. London: Gerald Duckwort & Co. Ltd.

Whitehead, N.E. (2007). An antiboy antibody? Re-examination of the maternal immune hypothesis. Journal of Biosocial Science, 39(6), 905-921.

Wikipedia. (2013). Blanchard's transsexualism typology.
http://en.wikipedia.org/wiki/Blanchard's_transsexulaism
_typology

Wikipedia. (2013). Causes of transsexualism.
http://en.wikipedia.org/wiki/Causes_of_transsexualism

Wikipedia. (2013). Gender Identity Disorder.
http://en.wikipedia.org/wiki/Gender_identity_disorder

Wikipedia. (2013). History of violence against LGBT people
in the united states.
http://en.wkipedia.org/wiki/History_of_violence_against_
LGBT_people_in_the_United_States

Wikipedia. (2013). Homosexual behavior in animals.
http://en.wikipedia.org/wiki/Homosexual_behavior_in_a
nimals

Wikipedia. (2013). Homosexuality.
http://en.wikipedia.org/wiki/Homosexuality

Wikipedia. (2013). List of animals displaying homosexual
behavior.
http://en/wikipedia.org/wik/List_of_animals_displaying_
homosexual_behavior

Wikipedia. (2013). Sexual orientation.
http://en.wikipedia.org/wiki/Sexual_orientation

Wikipedia. (2013). Social construction.
http://en.wikipedia.org/wiki/Social_constructionism

Wikipedia. (2013). Transgender.
http://en.wikipedia.org/wiki/Transgender

Williams, F.E. (1936). Papuans Of The Trans-Fly. London:
Oxford University Press.

Wilson, E.O. (1978). On Human Nature. Cambridge, MA:
Harvard University Press.

Wrangham, R.W. (1986). Ecology and social relationships in
two species of chimpanzee. In D.I. Rubenstein, & R.W.
Wrangham (Eds), Ecological Aspects Of Social Evolution:

Birds And Mammals. Princeton, New Jersey: Princeton University Press.

Yamagiwa, J. (1987). Intra and inter group interactions of an all-male group of virunga mountain gorillas (gorilla gorilla beringei). Primates, 28(1), 1-30.

Yamamoto, D., Ito, H., & Fujitani, K. (1996). Genetic dissection of sexual orientation: Behavioral, cellular, and molecular approaches in drosophilia melanogaster. Neuroscience Research, 26(2), 95-107.

Zeiss, A.M., Rosen, G.M., & Zeiss, R.A. (1977). Orgasm during intercourse: A treatment strategy for women. Journal Of Consulting And Clinical Psychology, 45, 891-895.

Zhou, J.N., Hofman, M.A., Gooren, L., & Swaab, D.F. (1995). A sex difference in the human brain and its relationship to transsexuality. Nature, 378(6552), 68-70.

Zucker, K.J., & Bradley, S.J. (1995). Gender Identity Disorder And Psychosexual Problems In Children And Adolescents. New York: Guilford.

Index

9 781596 301023